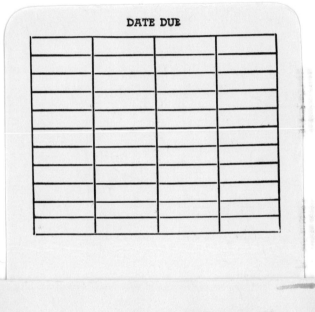

DATE DUE

Washoe

Reading, Writing, Chattering Chimps

Lana

Sarah

Sarah

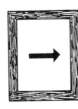

please

.machine

come

Elizabeth

Peony

is

plural

large

Reading

into

room

tickle

period

Writing, Chattering Chimps

TEXT AND DRAWINGS BY ALINE AMON

ATHENEUM   NEW YORK   1975

Drs. Beatrice T. and
R. Allen Gardner
DEPARTMENT OF PSYCHOLOGY
UNIVERSITY OF NEVADA
RENO, NEVADA

Library of Congress
Cataloging in Publication Data

Amon, Aline.
Reading, writing, chattering chimps.
SUMMARY: Text and pictures describe the many ways
chimpanzees are being taught to communicate with men.
   1. Chimpanzees—Behavior—Juvenile literature.
2. Animal communication—Juvenile literature.
[1. Chimpanzees—Habits and behavior. 2. Animal
communication] I. Title.
QL737.P96A46   001.5   75-9524
ISBN 0-689-30472-2

The photo on page 9 from *The Mind of the Dolphin* by John
Cunningham Lilly, M.D. Copyright © 1967 by John Cunningham
Lilly. Reproduced by permission of Doubleday & Company, Inc.

Published simultaneously in Canada by
McClelland & Stewart, Ltd.
Manufactured in the United States of America by
Halliday Lithograph Corporation
West Hanover, Massachusetts
First Edition

Dr. David Premack
CENTER FOR ADVANCED STUDY IN
THE BEHAVIORAL SCIENCES
STANFORD, CALIFORNIA

Dr. Roger S. Fouts
DEPARTMENT OF PSYCHOLOGY
UNIVERSITY OF OKLAHOMA
NORMAN, OKLAHOMA

Acknowledgements

With grateful appreciation for the generous cooperation of the scientists leading the research into communication between species, without which there would be no book—and no "talking" animals.

Also deserving warm thanks for their contributions are Dr. Philip Ogilvie, Executive Director, Portland Zoological Gardens, Portland, Oregon, for photographs and information on the chimpanzee training program at the Zoo; Timothy Gill, Emory University, Atlanta, Georgia, for providing some of the lexigram designs; Ellen Arntz, Santa Barbara, California, for Sarah's symbols; Francine Patterson, Stanford University, for the photograph of Koko, the gorilla; Jean and Robert Henning, Brooklyn, New York, for the picture of Nina; Murray Zaret, Animal Nursery, Brooklyn, for the loan of his chimpanzees for photographs and the hand outline; Lauren Goodrich, for modeling the Ameslan "Smile"; and Niel Goodrich, for help in the darkroom and studio.

Dr. Duane M. Rumbaugh
CHAIRMAN, DEPARTMENT OF PSYCHOLOGY
GEORGIA STATE UNIVERSITY
ATLANTA, GEORGIA

Contents

For Lauren Aline Goodrich

A familiar fairy-tale villain leads Red Riding Hood astray, while . . .

Talking Animals—
Fact or Fiction?

Did you ever wish you could talk *with* your dog, not just say *to* him "Sit" or "Come"? People have always been fascinated by the idea of talking animals. Fairy stories tell of beasts and birds who share helpful secrets with people, and books for little children are filled with friendly, chattering mice and rabbits. Sly foxes talk easily in fables written years ago for adults. In pioneer times tall tales traded around campfires told of dogs and mules much wiser than their masters. Today the television screen is alive with talkative cartoon creatures.

Once people really believed that some animals could speak. In Europe up until the eighteenth century people thought the devil gave animals that power. Owners of talking dogs were burned as witches. Frightened peasants stoned an Italian nobleman's whippet to death because it was supposed to know eight words in French and fifteen in Italian.

. . . a possum and a porcupine ponder pollution in "Pogo."

Fear of the devil disappeared, but reports of talking dogs continued. The most common stories were about animals who recited the alphabet or said **coffee, tea** or **chocolate**—or just **hunger**—in the different languages of their masters. One dog was trained by a farmhand, who held and poked its neck to help it form words. Reports say that this dog was given to a duke so that its "conversations" could amuse the noble and his court.

As a boy, Alexander Graham Bell tried to teach his Skye terrier to speak the same way. While the dog growled, he shaped its throat with his hands. "How are you, Grandma?" was the animal's most successful sentence, but it sounded more like **Ow ah oo gwah mah.** Bell's interest in speech later led him to a lifetime of work helping the deaf, and to many inventions, including the telephone.

In the early twentieth century, a German pointer

named Don performed on stages in Europe and the United States, repeating his eight-word vocabulary in theaters and lecture halls. Although his speech was hoarse and blurred, newspaper reports called it understandable, with a little help from the imagination of the audience.

These clever dogs were trained to "speak" the way other dogs are trained to sit up or to play dead. Talking was a harder trick for them to learn, though, since imitating human sounds was an unnatural act for them. And the words they produced did not lead to real conversations between pets and their masters.

Sea mammals are other creatures that men have imagined might be able to speak. Ancient Greek literature tells of singing dolphins. Pliny, a Roman writing in the first century, believed that a seal would answer in a loud voice if called by its name. The problem was discovering a seal's name in the first place.

A nineteenth century book about animal behavior told

of a sea lion, performing at fairs, with a four-word vocabulary: **Mama**, **Papa**, **yes** and **no**. Carl Hagenbeck, an early trapper and trainer, as well as the founder of a famous zoo in Germany, claimed he had a talking walrus, but that animal only said **Papa**.

Whether or not dolphins "sing," they are certainly intelligent and friendly toward people. There are many stories of dolphins guiding ships and rescuing drowning humans. One dolphin came daily to a beach in New Zealand for several months in 1955 to play with the children there. Opo, as she was called, enjoyed games of tag, fetch-

A "talking fish," really a seal, performs before an audience in an engraving from an 1859 issue of Harper's Weekly.

the-ball or ring-around-the-dolphin. Her special friend was a thirteen-year-old girl, Joy. Opo swam out to sea with Joy on her back. Then she tumbled her friend into the water and the girl and the dolphin raced each other back to the beach. Crowds came to watch, and the government passed a law just to protect Opo. Unhappily, she died the same day the law came into effect. Three boys using dynamite to catch fish accidentally killed Opo, too.

Captive dolphins are trained to catch balls, jump through hoops, ring bells and perform other tricks to amuse audiences. Dr. John C. Lilly, a physiologist and marine biologist, believed that they could also be taught to talk with humans. In 1959 he set up the Communication Research Institute on St. Thomas, one of the American Virgin Islands. He lowered microphones into tanks holding dolphins and recorded their sounds on tape. The tapes showed that the animals were imitating their keepers' laughter and the rhythm of their speech, but in much higher tones. Many animals, dogs and birds as well as dolphins, are able to hear sounds too high for the human ear. Dr. Lilly's dolphins seemed to understand this, and lowered their voices until they could be heard by people.

The most serious attempt at teaching dolphins to speak was carried out by Margaret Howe, an assistant of Dr. Lilly. She actually lived for two and a half months in a flooded room with a dolphin named Peter, talking to him loudly and frequently. Dr. Lilly hoped that the dolphin and the woman might learn to communicate with each other if they had no other company. The water in the room was just deep enough to allow Peter to swim, but shallow

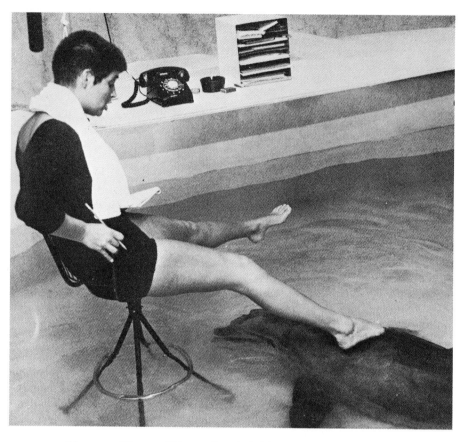

Margaret Howe talking to her dolphin roommate, Peter.

enough for Miss Howe to wade. Her bed, telephone, records and other things that had to stay dry were kept on platforms at the sides of the room. Miss Howe had one or two days off each week to escape her soggy surroundings. The rest of the time she kept busy playing ball and other games with Peter, scratching him, talking to him, keeping notes and recordings of the experiment—and cleaning up the pool.

At first Peter was noisy when Miss Howe was speaking. She had to train him to be quiet and listen to her. Dr. Lilly and Miss Howe divided Peter's noises into two types—"delphinese" for the clicks, squeaks, rasps, whistles and other sounds typical of dolphins, and "humanoid" for those more like human speech. Peter did not have much trouble imitating the pattern of his trainer's speech, giving out as many bursts of sound as the syllables in her sentences. But he never formed words. By the end of the experiment, and probably of Miss Howe's patience, Peter was keeping quiet while she spoke and repeating the rhythm of her sentences with more humanoid sounds than delphinese ones. It was only rarely, though, that his answers included sounds such as **ow** or **aw**, imitating Miss Howe's "clown" and "ball."

No one knows if dolphins can really be trained to talk, instead of just mimicking speech like Peter. It seems very unlikely, because dolphins have no vocal chords. They must make the humanoid sounds through their blowholes. And talking dogs are just cleverly trained to imitate speech without understanding it, so we still need growls or wagging tails to tell us what a dog is thinking. But people are carrying on real conversations with another animal—the chimpanzee.

Moses, Gua
and Viki

We have always been curious about our nearest animal relatives, the great apes. Chimpanzees are particularly interesting because they look like "furry little men." They can learn to do many of the things people do—eat with a fork and knife, drink from a cup, use the bathroom and, in the circus, play ice hockey and ride motorcycles. Early explorers in Africa mention tame chimpanzees grinding grain with stones, bringing water from rivers and frightening monkeys away from rice fields, while captured animals being shipped to England and Europe helped sailors handle the vessels' ropes. A French naval officer in the 1700s wrote that the African natives felt "that it is only from idleness that he (the chimpanzee) refrains from speaking, or perhaps from the fear of being made to work."

As the years passed, men in close contact with chimpanzees naturally wondered if they could be trained to "speak."

At the end of the nineteenth century, Richard L. Garner spent a great deal of time listening to monkeys in zoos, trying to understand the noises they made.

Since he was also interested in the sounds of the great apes, which were rare in captivity at that time, Mr. Garner then went to Africa. There he spent about three and a half months living in a wire-mesh cage in the jungle, so that he could overhear the wild animals in safety. The cage, named "Fort Gorilla," held a hammock, chair, table and the necessary clothing, food, camera equipment, tools and guns. Ants and other insects acted as dishwashers, cleaning plates that Mr. Garner left in the bush after his meals.

Mr. Garner decided that there were twenty-five to thirty different sounds that could be called the "words" of a chimpanzee language. Although chimps answered him when he copied one of these sounds, he never understood what they were trying to tell him.

Mr. Garner also tried to teach human words to a baby chimp, Moses, who had been found alone in a swamp. Moses was allowed to climb freely about the jungle, but he stayed near the cage and joined his human friend inside it for meals, companionship and naps in a hammock hung next to his master's. Mr. Garner repeated words over and over while the little animal sat in his lap and stared up at him in confusion. Finally, the ape began to move his lips, and he mouthed **Mama**, but without sound. Mr. Garner claimed he did learn to say **feu** (French for "fire") and **wie** (German for "how"), and to recognize **nkgwe** ("mother" in an African language). No wonder he never could pronounce that one!

Richard L. Garner in "Fort Gorilla."

Mr. Garner did not need all these languages to understand his little pet, though. Moses made repeated and recognizable signs with his hands for "no" and "yes."

Another primate, a female orangutan from Borneo, was chosen as a pupil by Dr. William H. Furness III in the early 1900s. After six long months of training, she could say only one word, **Papa**. Dr. Furness repeated the word while shaping his student's lips. Sometimes he held up a mirror so that she could see what she was doing.

For the next word, Dr. Furness pushed the orang's tongue against the back of her throat with a tongue depressor and held her nostrils shut with his other hand. She breathed out **ka**. By pinching her lips together at the end of the sound, Dr. Furness turned it into **cup**. The orang understood her two words. She patted her teacher on his shoulder when asked "Papa?" and called for her **cup** when she was thirsty. Unfortunately, the orangutan died suddenly before she could be taught more English.

In 1930, Dr. Winthrop N. Kellogg decided to bring up a baby chimp in his home with his ten-month-old son, Donald. He wanted to see how the child and chimpanzee would differ if they were reared exactly the same way. He borrowed a seven-and-a-half-month-old female chimpanzee named Gua from the Anthropoid Experiment Station in Orange Park, Florida. Both babies led the same life and they played together happily: follow-the-leader, tag, peek-a-boo and jumping from the couch onto pillows, a game invented by Gua. They dug in the sand, built with blocks and pulled each other around in a wagon. The little ape, stronger and quicker, was best at running, jumping and

Donald Kellogg and his furry friend, Gua, play together with blocks.

chasing. Donald had more patience and was better at picking up small objects. The Kelloggs felt that one-year-old Gua had the mental ability of a child the same age, but the agility of a four-year-old and the strength of an eight-year-old.

The chimp and child were often tested to compare their abilities. But they did not receive any special training, since the Kelloggs were recording their natural growth. The one thing Dr. Kellogg did try to teach Gua was the word **Papa**. He repeated the word to the ape while she was lying on her back in his lap. The lessons lasted for several months but Gua, while enjoying the attention, never tried to say **Papa**. The little chimp made no effort to copy

English. She could make her wishes known by her sounds and actions. When Gua grasped someone's hand, she was asking to be swung, while pushing out her lips meant that she wanted a drink.

Donald also made little effort to speak. Instead, he began to imitate his companion's chimpanzee food grunts. The boy could only say three words at the time he was seventeen months old, an age when some children know fifty. After he could walk upright, he went back to moving on all fours, like his furry playmate. The experiment ended when the friendly, but wordless, chimp was sent back to the Station so that Donald could catch up with human habits.

Almost twenty years later, the Anthropoid Experiment Station gave another chimpanzee to a human family. By then the Station was known as the Yerkes Laboratory of Primate Biology. The lab was named for Dr. Robert M. Yerkes. When he founded it in 1930, Dr. Yerkes established the first large collection of primates in the United States to be used for breeding and scientific studies.

Viki was only six weeks old when she went to live with Cathy Hayes and her husband, Keith, a research psychologist at the Yerkes Lab. Mrs. Hayes had been caring for the four-pound baby in the nursery of the Lab since she was three days old. The Hayeses had to find an apartment where apes were welcome tenants, though, before they could bring the baby home in a picnic basket. Viki was a scrawny, scared little infant who looked like a furry spider.

She quickly grew into a clever and very active ape, climbing, jumping and swinging constantly. She paddled in a fishpond, turned on faucets for a drink and caught raindrops on her tongue. In the sizzling Florida summers she tried to escape the heat by climbing into the refrigerator. Imitating Mrs. Hayes, Viki polished mirrors and beat cake batter. She pedaled her tricycle—with her hands—and played with her cash register, balls, guitar and many other toys. Viki also experimented with the family's typewriter, telephone and tools. She became a skillful pickpocket and busy bulb-snatcher. The chimp enjoyed scribbling with just about anything—either end of a pencil, crayons, soap and pickles—on just about anything—paper, books, walls and floors. If a windowpane became clouded with moisture, Viki even drew on that with her finger. When given pictures of people and of chimpanzees to sort, the confident little ape put all the humans in one pile and all the chimps in another—but she added her own picture to the people pile!

Viki advanced physically much more rapidly than a human baby, but the only sounds she made were occasional grunts or hoots. The Hayes decided to try to teach her to speak by methods used with children who have trouble talking. They tempted her into making a noise when she wanted her food by showing it to her, stirring it and even feeding each other. With difficulty, the chimp produced an **aahhhh** sound, which earned her the food. She had to strain to make this rasping noise because it was the first time she had willed herself to vocalize. Her hoots, grunts and screams were natural chimpanzee responses to pleasure, anger or fear. Her **ahh** was unnatural and forced. But Viki began to use it when she asked for toys or attention as well as for food. Mrs. Hayes waited four months before any further training. She hoped that **ahh** might become easier for the chimp to say—or, at least, more pleasant for humans to hear!

When neither of these happened, Mrs. Hayes went ahead with her plans to teach Viki **Mama**. At first she pressed the chimp's lips together while the ape breathed out **ahh**. Later, just a fingertip on her lip was enough to

Fingers on her lips help Viki pronounce **Mama**.

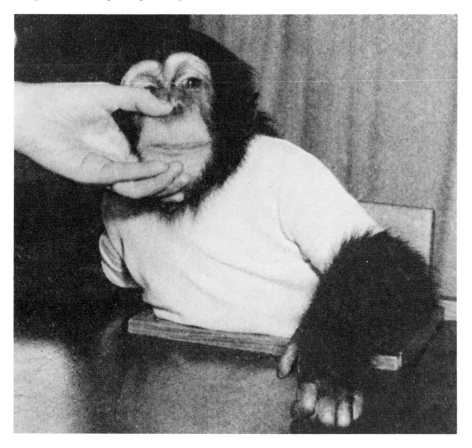

help Viki say **Mama**. Even after she no longer needed this human touch, the chimp continued to put her own finger on her upper lip.

The Hayeses had been training Viki with what they called the "Imitation" or "Do This" game. They blew whistles, clapped their hands or patted their heads while telling the chimp to "Do this!" Viki copied them and earned jelly beans or marshmallows. Eventually the Hayes added mouth movements and sounds to the actions Viki had to imitate. All chimps make a sound like the rude, human "Bronx cheer," an explosive puffing out of breath through lips in the "p" position. Mrs. Hayes asked the little ape to "Do this," and gave a Bronx cheer. For two months she continued to produce the sound, but always in a slightly quieter and shorter form. When Viki was almost two years old, the only syllables left in it were **Papa**, her second word.

Another sound practiced during the "Do This" game was **k**. When Mrs. Hayes was talking with a friend about the possibility of teaching Viki **cup**, since the chimp already knew the **k** and **p** sounds, Viki imitated them and produced the word by herself. Although she sometimes mixed up **Mama** and **Papa**, there was no question about her understanding **cup**. The thirsty chimp repeated it as often as 100 times a day!

Cup was Viki's best word. Her **Mama** was sometimes closer to a breathy **Ha-ha**, and **Papa** sounded like two smacking kisses. Viki did not speak easily, but wriggled and twisted while struggling to say her three words. While she was practicing a fourth one, **up**, she died of pneumonia, at the age of six and a half.

Why Chimps?

These experiments were not very encouraging. No ape had mastered more than four words, and some took as long as six years to learn that much. Six-year-old children are already off to school, talking busily all day long and ready to read and write. Many scientists were sure that chimpanzees simply lacked the mental ability to understand language. They felt that language and intelligence belonged together. No creature less intelligent than human beings could use words and build sentences.

A physical reason for the apes' inability to speak, however, was discovered by Dr. Philip Lieberman of the University of Connecticut. He noticed that the underdeveloped lower jaw of a chimpanzee was very much like the small bottom jaw of a newborn baby. A study showed that both apes and infants had vocal tracts quite different from those of older children and adults.

Our voices come from the larynx, or "voice box," in the throat. Air passing through the vocal cords in this voice box causes them to vibrate and make a noise, just as guitar strings do after they have been plucked. This noise travels up the throat into the pharynx, the space that connects passages from the stomach and lungs to the mouth and nose. The pharynx changes its shape slightly as many as ten times just to turn a sound from the vocal cords into the vowels "a" or "i." But the pharynxes of newborn babies and chimpanzees are too narrow and rigid to do this. The newborn baby's vocal tract starts to change after about six weeks, but that of a chimpanzee never gains the flexibility

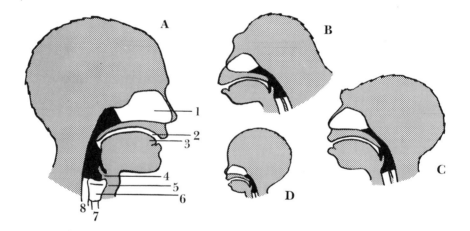

Comparison of the broad, angular pharynx area (in black) of an adult man (A) with the narrow, sloping tubes of an adult chimpanzee (B), Neanderthal man (C) and newborn infant (D). 1—the nasal cavity; 2—the oral cavity; 3—the tongue; 4—the epiglottis, which closes over the windpipe during the act of swallowing; 5—the vocal cords; 6—the larynx; 7—the trachea, or windpipe, to the lungs; and 8—the esophagus leading to the stomach.

needed for all the different sounds of human speech. The resemblance between the jaws of apes and those of primitive people also suggested that early Neanderthal man made only wordless noises—barks and grunts.

Also unlike human beings, chimpanzees do not normally use their lips and tongues to form their sounds. Dr. Furness had to push Gua's tongue back, and Mrs. Hayes had to hold Viki's lips together.

Unless coaxed and trained, chimps never try to copy speech, although they delight in mimicking other human actions. The sounds the apes do make—hoots, pants, grunts, whimpers, barks and screams—are always in answer to some special situation—meeting another chimp, sighting food or sensing danger. Without something like that to "talk" about, both wild and captive chimpanzees are usually silent. Dogs and other animals also only "vocalize" in certain situations. An excitable poodle will bark if a doorbell rings, but not just as a conversational greeting to his master in the morning.

All these facts seemed to prove that people and chimpanzees could never speak together. However, other habits of the apes suggested to some scientists another way to communicate with the animals—sign language. Wild chimps make a few signs among themselves in the forest. Puzzled animals scratch their heads as a person might. Frightened ones touch each others' lips repeatedly to build up their courage. In some tribes a leader stops his fellows with a raised hand, like a policeman directing traffic. Captive chimps hold out their hands to their keepers begging for food. Viki accompanied her few words with the same gestures whenever she spoke. Films of her talking can be understood even without the sound track.

Chimpanzees are also able to use their hands cleverly. Tame ones quickly learn to turn keys in locks and escape if they have the chance. They can build with blocks, put coins in slot machines and play tic-tac-toe by pushing levers. Wild chimps use twigs to dig honey from bees' nests or

Fifi, one of the chimpanzees observed by Jane van Lawick-Goodall at the Gombe Stream Reserve in Tanzania, pokes into a termite mound with a blade of grass, fishing for the edible insects.

Jezebel, at the Portland Zoo, Oregon, uses tools to paint. She also makes them.

tasty termites from their mounds. They wave sticks and throw stones at their enemies. The twigs, sticks and stones could be called the chimpanzees' tools.

Apes are the only tool-*using* animals in the wild, except for sea otters and a few species of birds. And chimpanzees are the only tool-*making* animal known except for humans. Jane Lawick-Goodall, watching groups of chimpanzees in Africa, saw them crush and chew leaves. When the leaves were as absorbent as sponges, the thirsty chimps stuck them into tree holes to soak up the water caught there.

Chimpanzees at the zoo in Portland, Oregon, do a similar thing. Paintings by these apes are sold to provide money for enriching the lives of the captive chimps. These animal artists chew paper towels until spongy, and useful in their painting efforts.

People use tools, people make tools and people speak languages. At one time human beings thought that these abilities separated them from the lower animals. Then it was discovered that chimpanzees can make and use simple tools. Could they also learn a simple version of human language?

In the last few years several scientists have tried again to communicate with chimpanzees, but this time in *visual* languages depending on sight, instead of a *vocal* language, which uses sound. And they have succeeded. Reports of talented apes are coming from all across the country. Washoe and Lucy and others "talk" with their hands, Sarah "writes" with symbols, and Lana communicates through a computer.

Washoe Comes to Washoe County

What is the difference between animal and human intelligence? And just how does someone learn a language? Would watching a chimpanzee learn sign language give some answers to these questions? Two psychologists, Doctors Beatrice and Allen Gardner, thought it might. They decided that they would try to teach the signs used by the deaf to a baby chimp.

Washoe, a little female born in Africa, arrived at the University of Nevada in June 1966. The Gardners guessed that she was between eight and fourteen months old, at about the same stage of development as a one-year-old child. The University is in Washoe County, so they named the infant ape Washoe.

The Gardners planned to compare Washoe's development with that of both normal children and deaf ones, who also had to communicate in signs. But children usually

A very new arrival to Washoe county, the infant ape looks out from under her blanket.

grow up in homes surrounded by the objects they learn to name—toys, pets, books, bottles, blankets, food and flowers. They constantly hear their parents' voices and see their gestures. They do not live in bare cages. Any poor baby brought up alone behind bars would develop much more slowly than other children. He might never speak at all. He would have no one to talk to and nothing to say.

The Gardners had to give Washoe as interesting a life as possible if they hoped to compare her with children. The ape needed toys and books and people and games to name with her signs. So Washoe lived in her own trailer behind the Gardners' house. The eight-by-twenty-four-foot trailer had a living room, kitchen, bedroom and bath. It stood in a large, 5,000 square-foot yard where there were jungle gyms and other outdoor playthings, as well as flowers, trees, bushes and gardening equipment. The hose became a plaything, too, when Washoe aimed it at her friends and drenched them with water. Inside, cabinets held the cleaning things and tools needed in every home, and Washoe's clothes, blankets, brushes and toys. There was also a full refrigerator!

Washoe had no chimpanzee companions. Chimps were hard to get, and the Gardners thought it best to start working with Washoe immediately. They were not even sure they could teach sign language to one animal.

Graduate students from the university worked as research assistants on the Gardners' project. They became the chimpanzee's caretakers, friends, teachers and disciplinarians. They played music to amuse her, but also frightened the curious chimp from forbidden places with burglar alarms and boat horns.

Washoe was fascinated by picture books and magazines. She found the pictures so real at first that she tried to pick flowers off the pages. The research assistants put together scrapbooks of her favorite pictures, which she looked through by herself as well as with human friends.

The students took Washoe on short trips to give her even more experiences. She played in country fields and romped in the university nursery school and playgrounds—but only on weekends, when there were no children to excite her. And no children to be excited by a visiting chimpanzee!

When Washoe arrived, she was a very little ape with

big, round eyes in a small, wrinkled face. She could climb trees and hang from branches by just one arm, but on the ground she behaved more like the baby she really was. She crawled on all fours, often tugging a blanket along behind her. Like all babies, Washoe used her hands awkwardly and slept a lot. Whenever she was awake, a trainer or two would be in the trailer with her, making signs. Like a child beginning to speak, she started slowly, learning only four signs during the first seven months of her training—**come-gimme, more, up** and **sweet**. After another seven months she knew nine more signs. Then she began to progress more quickly. She added twenty-one new signs during the third seven-month period. When she was about three, after twenty-one months of training, Washoe had a vocabulary

Washoe still enjoyed "reading" her magazines when she was five years old.

of thirty-four signs. This was much less than a three-year-old child would know, but it made scientific history. An animal was communicating with humans at last!

Her trainers used sign language among themselves as well as with the infant chimp, so that Washoe would not decide signs were "baby talk" meant just for her. This also helped the students. None of them had known sign language before, and they had to learn and teach at the same time. They never spoke aloud in the trailer, for fear Washoe might come to understand English and pay no attention to the signs she was supposed to learn. The chimp's human companions did make sounds though, but only wordless ones that Washoe could copy—clapping and drumming and noises showing happiness or disapproval. And they laughed, because chimpanzees laugh, too.

Some signs used by the deaf stand for the letters of the alphabet. Others take the place of a complete word, or even ideas that would need several words to express in English. These letters and signs can be combined to form two quite different languages. One is American Sign Language, or Ameslan. The signs are not put together like English sentences, but in the quickest and most concentrated way possible to convey the meaning. Students of Ameslan consider it a separate language, with rules and a "vocabulary" of its own. Like French or Chinese, it can be translated into English, but it is not based on it.

The second language is Signed English, or Siglish. The Siglish alphabet and signs are used in the sentence order of English. The alphabet is especially important for spelling out words for which there are no signs. Deaf persons are apt to learn Ameslan first, since it is meaningful for them, while spoken English is not. Siglish bridges the gap between the two languages and helps the deaf person learn English, almost as a second language.

In either language, signs can be a picture of the word (Washoe pulled the hair on her cheek outward to show a **cat's** whiskers); they can demonstrate an action involved with the word (for **baby**, Washoe folded her forearms together as if cradling a child); or they can be signs that do not describe the word in any way, but just stand for it. (With her fingers spread out, Washoe touched her nose with her thumb for **bug**—a gesture like a rude one children have been making for years.)

When the Ameslan signer gestures "What name," he indicates "your" by looking directly at the person he is asking. The quizzical expression on his face shows it is a question.

The Siglish signer makes gestures for the entire sentence, "What i-s your name."

From Babbling
to Ameslan

Her trainers surrounded Washoe with signs from the moment she arrived, before she could understand or copy them, like a mother chatting to an infant too young to speak. The baby hears the sounds for months. When he is ready, he imitates them.

Like a baby cooing and babbling and playing with noises, Washoe, after a few months of seeing the busy hands of her human companions, began to experiment with hers. At first, her gestures were not signs, but as meaningless as a baby's gurgles. The student teachers smiled and clapped to encourage these infant efforts, called "manual babbling" by the Gardners.

When a baby makes a sound like "Pa-pa-pa," his mother may repeat "Papa" and point to the father, trying to show the child that its sounds have a meaning. In the same way, when Washoe's teachers noticed her "babbling"

something close to an Ameslan sign, they copied the sign
and applauded her. They tried to invent situations that
would help the little ape understand her sign. Washoe de-
lighted in touching her friends' noses with her index finger,
a gesture close to the Ameslan **funny**, in which both index
and second fingers brush the side of the nose. So, laughing
all the while, the teachers turned nose-touching between
Washoe and themselves into a game. They started the game
whenever they saw a situation that might amuse a baby ape.
Eventually, Washoe made the sign herself to point out
something **funny** to her friends.

Washoe's babbling grew less as she learned more signs,
until after two years of training it was rare. Once she began to express herself in signs, her trainers no longer
encouraged random motions. If there seemed to be some
incomplete or incorrect sign in her gestures, the teachers
tried to correct it instead of applauding it, again like a

Running away is **funny** *to a chimp.*

mother unhappy with "Choo-choo" after her child has said "Train."

Washoe's teachers repeated over and over signs that matched the ape's activities. Every day, signs for **eat, drink, bed, bib, bath, hide** and **tickle** followed her through her daily routine of eating, drinking, bathing and playing games. Imitating, as all apes do, Washoe swept the floor and bathed her doll, and sometimes made the signs she saw for them.

One day, her trainers tried to give her an injection—without success. That was a game Washoe did not want to play. But later she even mimicked that unhappy experience. She pushed a nail against her leg as if it were the hypodermic needle.

One sign that Washoe learned through imitation was **sweet.** She craved sweet foods and, at that time, the only ones she received were desserts at the end of her meals. She greeted the sight of the baby-food jars with food barks and pleasure grunts. Her trainers made quite a ceremony of bringing the desserts while signing **sweet** repeatedly by touching their lips or tongues with the first and second fingers of one hand. In her first attempts to copy the sign, Washoe grabbed her tongue between the two fingers. After that, her teachers would not give Washoe the dessert until she had asked for it with some form of the sign. In less than a year, the chimpanzee was making the sign correctly not only for desserts, but also for candy and soda, her rewards for proper signing. She even pointed out pictures of them in her books as **sweet.**

Washoe also saw and copied signs that did not have

eat (food)   drink (cup)   tickle   bed

Ameslan usually has just one sign for a verb (eat) and a similar noun (food).

anything to do with her own activities. Although some chimpanzees are addicted to cigarettes, she was not allowed to smoke or handle matches. Some of the students, though, were heavy smokers. They signed to each other when they wanted to borrow a cigarette. One day her trainer was hunting for a match while Washoe watched with interest. To show the reason for the search, the teacher held the empty box out to Washoe. She answered with the **smoke** sign, and then continued to use it for matches, cigarettes and the boxes that held them.

The trainers could not rely only on imitation to teach Washoe new signs. It was hard to sign to her as often as a mother talks to her baby, since the research assistants might be too busy caring for her to use their hands for anything else. Or the active little ape might be high in a tree or hiding in a box, not watching for signs at all. A better way of training was called "molding." The students shaped her hands into the sign they were teaching, or one they were correcting. If she made a mistake in a new sign, they repeated the sign again and again, rewarding Washoe as her gesture grew closer to Ameslan. If the mistake was in a sign that she should know, the teachers made the gesture for **sign**. It meant they could not understand and the chimp had to try again. Washoe was usually a friendly and cooperative ape, but when she became too upset by her trainer's corrections she sometimes ran away or threw a temper tantrum.

Sometimes Washoe invented her own sign. If it was close enough to an Ameslan sign, she was taught to change it slightly. Then she knew another sign. Her very first one, **come** or **gimme**, grew from her habit of stretching out her

A gesture for **gimme** *is natural for untrained apes in the wild—and in cages.*

hand to beg for food or company. After she was trained to move the hand toward herself, in a beckoning motion, Washoe's gesture became sign language.

When Washoe was eager for a treat or a trip, she sometimes shook her hand impatiently. Other chimps and young children do the same thing. Perhaps it was the beginning of the Ameslan **hurry**. Deaf people shake their hands too, but with the index and second fingers held out together, and the others curled in the palm. However, human signers understand the shaking of an open hand, which Washoe used.

Washoe also invented signs not based on gestures natural to apes. One time her trainer showed the hungry chimp her bib before dinner. She quickly signed **come-gimme** and **please**, but not **bib**. Since they had not been able to find **bib** in their sign-language dictionaries, the Gardners had chosen **napkin** for Washoe instead. She should have wiped her mouth with her hand at the sight of the bib. Instead the chimpanzee put her index fingers behind her neck and then brought them down her chest and together, drawing the shape of her bib. The Gardners and the research assistants were excited by Washoe's clever sign, but they decided against using it. After all, they were teaching a chimpanzee to speak—she was not teaching them! But they were surprised later when they finally learned the Ameslan sign for **bib**. It was the same as Washoe's.

Without help from her trainers, Washoe stretched the meanings of her signs by using them for more than one thing. After learning to pat her head for one special

hat, she then made the sign for caps and kerchiefs and all other head coverings. **Open** was first a request for one particular door to be opened—then any door or box—and even soda bottles or a water faucet.

When Washoe did not know how to point out something interesting, she made the sign for something similar. Before she learned **smell**, Washoe called every strong odor **flower**. At the distant sound of barking, she slapped her thigh repeatedly in the sign for **dog**.

The research assistants also helped Washoe express as many ideas as possible with her small vocabulary by using one gesture for a number of different objects. The **napkin** sign not only covered **bib**, but also **facial tissue, toilet paper, washcloth** and **handkerchief**.

smell   sweet   flower

Washoe
Wants "More"

The story of how Washoe learned the sign for **more** is a good example of the methods used in her training. First her teachers noticed a gesture natural to the chimp. Then they shaped her hands into a sign closer to Ameslan. They repeated and corrected the sign while Washoe tried to imitate as well as she could. When her trainers were sure that she understood it meant **more** in one situation, they practiced it in others. Finally, Washoe herself began to use it every time she wanted **more** of something.

Tickling was her favorite game. Her trainers noticed that she brought her arms together over the spot being tickled, and even over a place they just threatened to tickle. Then they waited for her to move her arms together *before* she got the tickling she craved. Whenever she made the gesture, she was rewarded—with **more** tickling.

After Washoe seemed to understand the sign, the

students changed it slightly, getting her to bring just the tips of her fingers together, the Ameslan **more**.

Correction, repetition and imitation followed until Washoe used **more** regularly, but only when she wanted to be tickled. Then her friends began to use it with another game—pushing her around in a laundry basket. And next with still another game—swinging the chimp by her arms. And again, with pillow fights. Washoe copied them and earned **more** games. On her own she began to demand **more** of everything—food, candy and soda as well as tickling and swinging.

More was among the first four signs Washoe learned. It asked for something, and so did the other three—**come-gimme**, **up** (for a piggy-back ride) and **sweet** (for her favorite foods). The first sign that Washoe made just for comment or conversation, not as a demand, was **toothbrush**. Whenever she finished a meal, her trainer made the sign by rubbing his finger along his teeth. In the beginning Washoe hated to have her teeth brushed, but she copied the sign and then used it by herself after her dessert. She even learned to brush her teeth. While exploring the bathroom during a visit to the Gardners' home, the curious ape found a mug full of the family's toothbrushes. Not asking for anything, but just telling her human companions what she had found, Washoe signed the once-hated **toothbrush**.

As soon as she knew about ten signs, Washoe began to combine them. She started with simple two-word thoughts like **Gimme sweet**, but a few months later added **you** and proper names. She was taught these signs when she tried to feed the students or push them toward water so that they

Even at five and a half, Washoe does not seem very happy when Susan Nichols brushes her teeth.

would drink. Washoe's teachers would not touch the water if she simply signed **Drink**, but they accepted her invitation after she put together **You drink**. The chimp also learned the important word **me**. When shown her reflection in a mirror, Washoe noted **That me Washoe**, brushing her hands forward past her ears. Her name in signs was **Big Ears**.

Many of her phrases Washoe copied from her trainers, but she also combined signs in her own ways to express her own ideas. She asked **Gimme tickle** long before her teachers used the signs in that order. They had never dreamed that a chimp would actually tickle a person, so no one had told Washoe **Gimme tickle**.

Washoe added objects to her sentences, **You tickle me Washoe.** She added what the Gardners called "appeal" words, **more, help, please** and **hurry.** Then came adjectives to describe the nouns. **Sweet drink** meant "soda" and **green slices** were "cucumbers." Washoe knew **up** and **down, in** and **out.** When eager to get into a locked playroom, she begged her trainer **Help key in.**

To test whether Washoe combined her signs in ways that made sense when presented with new conditions, a research assistant named Susan Nichols stepped on the chimp's rubber doll repeatedly and recorded her responses —**up Susan, Susan up, mine please up, gimme baby, please shoe, more mine, up please, please up, more up, baby down, shoe up, baby up, please more up** and **you up.** Washoe really wanted to rescue her doll in a hurry, but she never signed meaningless phrases such as **baby Susan** or **more shoe.** Everything she gestured either described her doll's unhappy position, **baby down,** or begged Susan—or her shoe—to do something about it!

please

green

hurry

slices

Washoe Passes
Her Tests

The Gardners needed records of how Washoe learned signs and under what circumstances she made them, for their studies of animal intelligence. These records could also be compared to records made of children learning a language. For the first six months, the students took notes of all the signs Washoe used and what prompted them. As her vocabulary grew and she signed more often, it became difficult to write down her output in such detail. The trainers began to use printed lists of all Washoe's vocabulary. When the chimp gestured, they could check her sign off quickly. Washoe was supposed to know a sign after it had been seen by three different observers. The sign was called "reliable" if the chimp used it for fifteen days in a row.

Sometimes Washoe would not make a certain sign for days or weeks. If she did not see a cow, for instance, there would be no reason for the chimpanzee to use that sign. So the research assistants started drills twice a day to see if she had forgotten any of her old vocabulary. A picture of a cow in one of her books might inspire the chimp to make that gesture. These drills did not include the teaching of new signs, though, for fear Washoe might be bored and refuse to work. At times she tried to get by with an old, familiar sign if it was close to a new one. She even copied motions that had nothing to do with the lesson, scratching her nose or chin if the teacher did.

One word that was hard to practice in the drills was **no**. Her trainers certainly did not want Washoe to answer **No** when they told her to do something necessary. If they told her to do something foolish, instead, like commanding **Eat** after giving her a bowl of rocks, the good-natured ape might just lick the rocks obediently, and not refuse with **No**.

Telling Washoe tall tales turned out to be the best way to get her to sign **No**. One time a teacher explained that there was a large dog with big teeth outside, a dog who liked to eat little chimps. Then he asked **You want go out now**? The answer was a firm and sensible **No**!

Records were kept of Washoe's combinations as well as of her single signs. Her trainers whispered into a tiny tape recorder every sign the chimp made during fifteen- or twenty-minute sample periods at meal or play times. Other scientists had written down similar samples of young children's conversations. The records of the small children's speech and the small chimp's could be compared. Like the children, Washoe grew more "talkative" with time. Fifty signs used during supper in the fall of 1968 became 150 a little over a year later.

You	want	go	out	now

One of the important purposes of a language is to tell someone about something he cannot see. The Gardners checked to see if Washoe could do this with "double-blind" tests. In these tests two people watched the chimpanzee name something that they could not see but she could. The "blind" observers then wrote down the signs they thought Washoe had used. After the test they compared their notes with a list of the actual objects shown to the chimp. If both testers agreed upon the sign the ape had made and it was the right one, Washoe passed her test. Because the observers did not know the objects, they could not give the chimp any hints by mistake.

At first the experimenter showed Washoe pictures on cards. Since this test could be done anywhere, it was also tried with children. But both chimp and children became restless with nothing to do but wait for the tester to display a card. The tests had to be short and infrequent.

Next the objects were placed in a box with one clear plastic side, through which Washoe could see the **hat** or the **doll**. But the chimpanzee became even more restless and wriggly, since she had to wait while the box was being filled and emptied. Washoe grew more interested, though, when the experimenter let her partly run the tests herself. The box was put into a cabinet with a door. When Washoe wanted to play the game, she opened the door and named the object. When she was not interested, the door stayed closed.

Before she could pace the tests herself this way, Washoe sometimes just ran away or stole the object from the box. After she had some control over the tests, the chimpanzee named ninety-nine objects in one long session that lasted from 9:00 in the morning until 4:30 in the afternoon, with time out for meals, naps and romps with the students.

Projecting slides into the cabinet from the rear turned out to be the best—and quickest—testing method. Washoe

Two observers, one behind a one-way glass window, watch Washoe sign **tree** *during one of the double-blind tests.*

could still time the tests by opening the door and seeing the picture only when she wanted to, but the slides could be replaced much more rapidly than real objects. Instead of just one toy **car** for Washoe to name, the trainers showed slides of all sorts of automobiles, trucks, jeeps and station wagons, which they had photographed in the University parking lot. A single **flower** could be replaced by pictures of roses, poppies, daisies and many other kinds. With the slide tests, Washoe identified as many as forty things in only thirty-five minutes.

The longest test Washoe took included 128 slides. There were four examples each of thirty-two different types of objects. For example, **bug** would be the right sign for a beetle, bee, ant and grasshopper, and **dog** named a dachshund, Collie, terrier and German shepherd. If Washoe used **bug** or **dog** or one of the other thirty signs just by chance, she would have accidentally hit on the right one only one time out of thirty-two, according to the law of averages. This means that if Washoe was making signs without knowing their meaning, she might name four of the one hundred and twenty-eight slides correctly. However, one observer decided Washoe used the right sign ninety-two times, and the other, ninety-one. The chimpanzee was telling her human friends what she saw.

While they were still testing Washoe with objects, the scientists had to use little toy cars and trees and other things in place of the real objects, which were too large to fit in the box, of course. Often Washoe called the small toys **baby**. Her most common mistake during all the tests was naming the picture or object with the sign for something similar. She was much more likely to call cheese **fruit** than **dog**. This proved that Washoe understood the idea of categories—that **fruit** had much more in common with **cheese** than with **dog**. But she might mix up **dog** with **cow**, because they both belonged in the same group, or category. They were both animals.

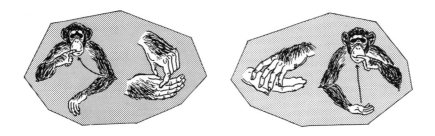

Categories. **Cereal** *and* **meat**. **Fork** *and* **spoon**

"Washoese"

When Washoe was five years old, she had a vocabulary of 132 Ameslan signs, plus a few others that were not part of the deaf language. When she wanted to play a game of hide-and-seek, she covered her eyes in a peek-a-boo gesture instead of copying her teachers' correct sign for **hide**. **Peek-a-boo** was not Ameslan, but it worked just as well as **hide**. No one could mistake the game Washoe wanted to play.

Washoe also understood several hundred more signs. Even this is far behind the language skill of a five-year-old child. Still, some of her development was like the change of a gurgling baby into a chattering child. Her "babbling" turned into "words," and the older she grew the more she "talked." She began to combine signs just before she was two, about the time children start to put words together. Very young children often place the noun before a word that describes it, perhaps because they learned the noun first. Washoe also signed **clothes white** or **baby mine** before she reversed the order to the **white clothes** used by her teachers. And again like very young people, Washoe used one sign, such as **dog**, for all animals until she knew the special one for each.

The Gardners felt that what they learned during Washoe's education might help them train other chimpanzees who would do even better. Although she had much more to do and see, and many more human friends, than most captive apes, Washoe still did not lead the life of a normal child. She was about a year old before her training started. By then, a baby has been listening to words for twelve long months. Washoe never had either another chimp or child her age to "chat" with in signs. Her chances to express whatever she wanted to her companions were also limited by all the drills and tests. In addition, the graduate students were not the best possible teachers of Ameslan because they were learning the signs too. A baby hears his mother talk easily in her own language, but Washoe only had a chance to sign with someone for whom Ameslan was an everyday language for two months during her second summer with the Gardners. At that time a fifteen-year-old boy named Dennis Schemenaur spent five or six hours a day "talking" with Washoe, helping her trainers and playing with the chimp. Washoe nipped Dennis when she first met him. It might have been a friendly gesture, since biting is a sign of affection among chimps in the wild. When she realized that humans did not enjoy being nibbled, though, Washoe and Dennis became good companions.

Chimpanzees' hands are much larger in proportion to

Dennis Schemenauer, wearing a party hat, asks Washoe to make the sign for it.

their bodies than ours. They are also shaped differently and move differently. A chimp can bend its hand so far forward that the palm touches the inside of the forearm, but it cannot bend the hand or fingers backward. Some of the nineteen different hand positions used in Ameslan were impossible for Washoe. For **flower**, the tips of the straight fingers and the thumb touch in what is called the "tapered" hand. Washoe's fingers were so long and her thumb so short that she could not bring the tips together without bending her fingers. She also substituted a loosely curved hand for both the Ameslan definitely curved and flat ones.

In Ameslan, **please** is expressed by rubbing a hand in a circle over the heart. Washoe simplified this and just passed her hand across her chest. Sometimes she brought her hands

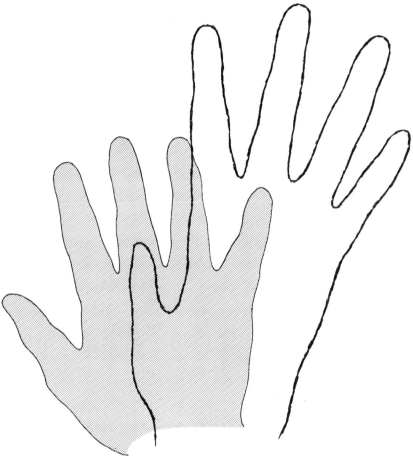

Outlines of the hands of an eight-month-old chimpanzee and a eight-month-old girl show the long fingers and short, weak thumb of the little ape.

The hands of a chimpanzee are much larger in proportion to its body than those of a man.

together over her head for **more**, instead of in front of her chest. Perhaps she wanted to be sure that the students noticed the sign, and held her hands up to them because she was so short. But her trainers understood and accepted these gestures. Even people using Ameslan do not always form signs in the same way. People in different parts of the country have different gestures, just as they have different spoken accents. Her teachers compared Washoe's signs to slang, and called them "Washoese."

When Washoe's phrases are written down they sound incomplete and ungrammatical, but she was a young animal. Little children also put sentences together using English words, but in a simplified way of their own.

Washoe's signing followed the rules of Ameslan more

closely than those of English. Short or unnecessary words like "is" or "and" were skipped and each idea was expressed as compactly and quickly as possible. For **No**, Washoe simply shook her head. Although there is another gesture for **No** in Ameslan, deaf people often just shake their heads, too, while their hands are busy shaping the words that **No** applies to. And Washoe did understand how the place of her signs in a sentence changed its meaning. She expected to be hugged if she asked **Roger hug Washoe**, and did the hugging herself after explaining **Washoe hug Roger**.

Some scientists may feel that Washoe did not really learn a language, but there can be no question that the animal was communicating with human beings. She carried on conversations with her companions like this one:

Roger:　**What you want?**
Washoe:　**Tickle**
Roger:　**Who tickle?**
Washoe:　**Dr. Gardner**
Roger:　**Dr. Gardner not here**
Washoe:　**Roger tickle**

She asked questions. When suppertime was near she motioned hopefully **Time eat?** The look on Washoe's face was enough to show that it was a question. After her trainer agreed that it was indeed time to eat, Washoe hooted with happiness and signed **Time eat!** with a very different expression on her face.

But Washoe was not always concerned with just fun and food. She was **sorry** after she had bitten someone, or

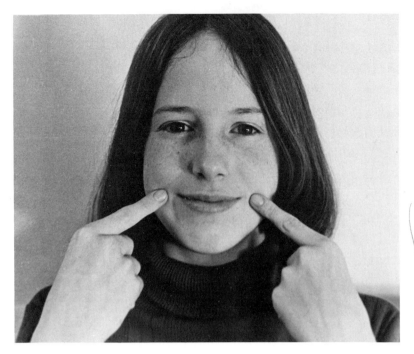

Smile *in Ameslan* . . .

even when it was not her fault that a student had been hurt. Once when Susan Nichols pretended to cry, Washoe scampered to her quickly to comfort her, signing **Hug hug.** When the chimp asked to be forgiven, she begged **Sorry sorry hug me good.** She commented **funny** during games or while her trainer chased her after she had been up to some mischief. After a doll had been put in her cup, she pointed out to her companions that **Baby in my drink.**

The clever chimp enjoyed playing with her signs and making jokes. She answered a question of Susan's in a spirit of fun:

Susan: **Who stupid?**
Washoe: **Susan stupid**

...and in Washoese.

Susan: **Who?**
Washoe: **Washoe stupid**

Washoe also used her new language by herself. She liked to look at her picture books alone, pointing out **That cat** or **That flower**. She even corrected herself when she made a mistake. If any of her teachers came too close during these times, she moved away and continued to "read" privately. When sneaking into a forbidden part of the yard, the naughty chimp warned herself **Quiet**.

When Washoe lay on her bed before going to sleep, she made signs, like a baby murmuring to itself as it relaxes. Her relaxation was a bit more athletic than a baby's, though. Sometimes she put a hat upside down on the bed, told herself **In** and then pushed her head into the hat, ending up by turning a somersault. Or she might put her red shoe on or pull it off, noting **That shoe** or **That red**.

Washoe took it for granted that everyone knew sign language, and even tried to sign with dogs and cats at first. When new students came to work with her, the chimp recognized, however, that they were not familiar with sign language. She made her signs very carefully and slowly to help the embarrassed beginners.

Usually Washoe formed her signs quickly. Despite her speed and slangy Washoese, a group of students in a school for the deaf who watched a movie of the chimpanzee "talking" understood her easily. Another time, two interested deaf people acted as observers for one of the double-blind tests. When they first watched Washoe, one understood sixty-seven percent of her signs and the other seventy-one percent. But the second time both of these new observers, at first unused to the chimpanzee version of sign language, accepted eighty-nine percent of her gestures. So Washoe could communicate not just with her trainers, but with many other people—with anyone who knew some sign language.

What would Washoe want if she made these signs?

Sarah's
"Plastic Language"

While Washoe was busily demanding sodas and candy in Ameslan, another chimpanzee was learning a different language in Santa Barbara, California. Dr. David Premack, of the Psychology Department at the University of California, was teaching Sarah, an African-born, six-year-old chimp, how to "read" and "write" with plastic symbols. Each symbol stood for a word. The plastic pieces had metal backs so that they would stick to a magnetized board. To earn her rewards, Sarah had to put the right symbols in the right order on the board. The ape herself chose to place the signs under each other, so that her sentences read from top to bottom, like those of the Chinese.

Dr. Premack hoped to teach Sarah not just the "words" of what he called her "plastic language," but also some of the grammatical rules of English, if she could understand them. The training program was carefully divided into simple steps, each one leading to the next. First came single "words" and then sentences, questions, "metalinguistics," features of objects (color, size, shape), compound sentences, plurals, amounts (all, none, some, several) and last, the meaning of if-then sentences (*if* something happens, *then* something else will follow).

Sarah did not have constant human company like Washoe. She worked with only one trainer during her lessons, and spent the rest of the time in her cage.

Words. Sarah's first lesson was based on an action natural for chimpanzees—giving. Even in the wild they give things to each other, and in captivity trainers give toys and food to their charges. Because of this, the first sentence the scientists decided to teach Sarah was **Mary give banana Sarah.**

In the only available photograph of Sarah, she is giving the symbol for **size-of** *to her trainer, Mary Morgan.*

Sarah could not learn the sentence until she knew all the symbols. Her teachers began with **banana**. Sarah and Mary, one of the research associates, sat at a table across from each other with a slice of the fruit between them. Mary smiled happily when Sarah took the banana. Then the teacher put a pink plastic square where the banana had been, and another slice out of Sarah's reach. The chimp had to put the square on the board before she got the faraway piece of fruit.

Before Sarah had learned that the pink square meant the long, yellow fruit, she understood that she might earn a treat by giving something else in exchange for what she wanted. One time Dr. Premack and another psychologist were sipping coffee outside her cage. Sarah had never tasted coffee, but she was curious. There were some rectangular monkey-food biscuits on a sink in her cage. The biscuits were about the same size as the symbols. Sarah picked up one of them and offered it to the scientists through the bars of her cage. It was easy to see what she wanted, and they let her have a sip of coffee. Sarah must have enjoyed it, for she then handed them one biscuit after another until they gave her a cup for herself.

The chimp learned more easily that a given plastic symbol meant just one kind of fruit when she had two different fruits to compare. **Apple** was paired with **banana**, and later **raisin** with **date**, **apricot** with **orange**, and so on.

In the same way, Sarah was introduced to several verbs when it was time for her to learn **give**. It was easier for her to understand the symbols if she saw the action that went with each one. If Sarah put **Give apple** on the board, the

Elizabeth, one of Sarah's successors, gives an apple to her trainer. Note the symbol for **Elizabeth** *hanging around her neck on a string.*

fruit was hers. But if the chimp wrote **Wash apple**, the teacher dunked it into a bowl of water.

Sentences. When Sarah was able to combine **Give banana** fairly regularly, she was not rewarded for the backward **Banana give** anymore. Her trainers were working toward the complete sentence in the right order.

To help the chimp learn names, both Sarah and her trainers wore the plastic symbols for their names around their necks on strings. When she knew the three words, **Mary give banana**, the chimp got no reward if she went back to using just two signs. After she had learned **Mary give banana Sarah**, she was not allowed to use only three symbols. Once, while she was practicing adding her name to the sentence, Sarah accidently wrote **Mary give banana Gussie**. Gussie, another chimpanzee, got the banana—and that was a mistake Sarah never made again!

Questions. When Sarah was given two cups and a spoon, she recognized that the cups were the same and put them together. Her trainers gave her many other sets of three objects, and she easily chose the two that matched. Then they placed a sign meaning **same** between two apples, and one for **different** between an apple and a banana. They put **same** between cups and **different** between a cup and a spoon. They continued to drill the chimpanzee, with keys, corks, paper clips and many other things, until she seemed to understand the signs.

Peony, another of Dr. Premack's students, also follows the instructions on the board and washes an apple.

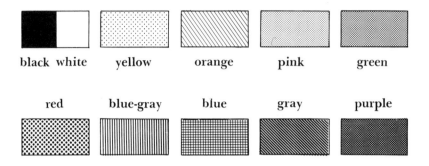

black white   yellow   orange   pink   green

red   blue-gray   blue   gray   purple

Sarah was taught **same** and **different** because these symbols made it easy to train her to answer questions. The students used a purple piece of plastic with a hole in it for a question mark. It showed that something was missing from a sentence. Sarah had to replace the **question** symbol with one that gave this missing information. **Apple question apple** asked what one apple was to another, and the right explanation was **Apple same apple**. Sarah was supplied with only the one sign, **same**, in the beginning so that she could not make a mistake. When her trainers thought Sarah knew that she had to remove the question piece and put another one in the sentence, they also gave her **different**. Then the chimp had to choose the correct answer from the two signs.

Sarah already knew the meaning of **no** from commands forbidding something—**Sarah no take cracker.** Now she learned **yes**, when that was the only sign she had to answer **Apple same apple question**. Throughout her training, Sarah was taught new symbols either by giving her two to compare with each other (**give, wash**) or by supplying only one sign for her to use until she understood it.

"Metalinguistics." Her trainers introduced two more matched "words" or ideas, **name-of** and **not name-of**. They

put the sign for **name-of** between the blue triangle that Sarah knew as **apple** and a real apple. When Sarah understood this sign, her training went more quickly. She could learn a symbol just by seeing **name-of** between the new plastic shape and the new object. For example, when she saw a small blue rectangle followed by **name-of** and a real apricot, Sarah learned **apricot**. The trainers were using one "word" (**name-of**) to teach the chimp another one (**apricot**). This system of teaching language with language itself is called "metalinguistics" by scientists. Later, even **name-of** could be omitted. Sarah learned new symbols when a student just held up the plastic piece and the object and shook them at the chimp.

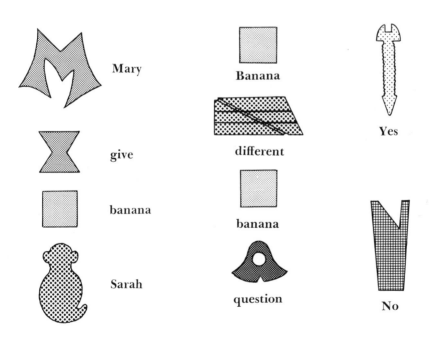

Words into sentences. Questions and answers

Features of objects. Sarah had already shown that she could recognize resemblances and differences. Now a toy car, a candy, a ball and other things were placed on her table. They had nothing in common with each other except their color—red. And Sarah had no symbol with which to describe them except the new **red.** Then the chimp practiced with groups of yellow objects until she could pick the right sign for a yellow balloon or a red feather from the two colors.

After Sarah had learned other symbols that described objects—**square** and **round, large** and **small**—she was taught the relationships between them and the object. Just as she realized that the blue triangle was the **name-of** an apple, Sarah now understood that **red** was the **color-of** the apple, **large** was the **size-of** the apple and **round** was the **shape-of** the apple.

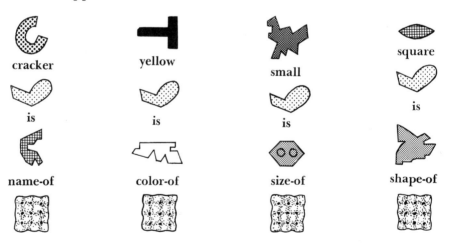

cracker	yellow	small	square
is	is	is	is
name-of	color-of	size-of	shape-of

*Features of objects: Sarah not only knew that the C-shaped symbol at the upper left was the **name-of** a cracker, but she could also describe its color, size and shape.*

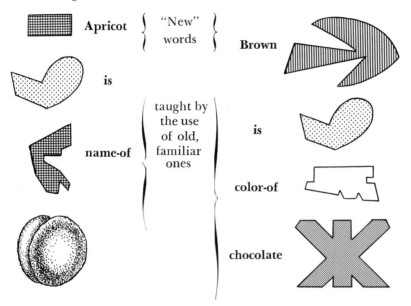

Apricot } "New" words { Brown

is

name-of } taught by the use of old, familiar ones { is

color-of

chocolate

This made teaching Sarah more colors much simpler. She knew the sign for **brown** right away after seeing the sentence **Brown is color-of chocolate.** The scientists did not use a round piece of plastic for the word **round** on purpose. And the pieces for **red, yellow** and **brown** were *not* red, yellow or brown. Sarah's language had to be as abstract as English. A child has to memorize what color "yellow" is. There are no clues in the word itself to tell him. In the same way, Sarah's symbols did not give her any hints about the color they represented.

Even though there was no chocolate to be seen when her teacher put **Brown is color-of chocolate** on Sarah's board—and the symbol for **brown** was blue-gray and the one for **chocolate** green—the chimp knew the color of her favorite candy. She proved it by choosing a brown disk from among four different colored ones when asked to by her trainer. She had learned **brown** through the use of **color-of.**

A Grammatical
Chimp

Plurals. Sarah's training even included a plural form of the verb to be used when the sentence had more than one subject. She could write a sentence that meant **Red and green are colors**, although she did not have a separate sign for **are**. Instead, one sign for **plural** was used with all verbs. Her symbols on the board would be **Red green is plural color**, or **Sarah Gussie insert plural cracker**. Sarah added the plural sign to a verb only when there were two subjects in the sentence, not when there were just two symbols before the verb, like **round ball**.

Compound sentences. Sarah was next taught to understand sentences with more than one idea. Her trainer first put two whole sentences on the board. Then she combined them by removing one sign at a time. **Sarah insert banana dish** and **Sarah insert apple pail** became **Sarah insert ba-**

Plurals

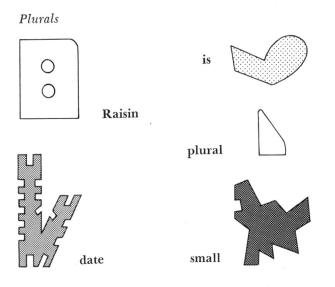

Raisin

is

plural

date

small

nana dish insert apple pail, and finally, **Sarah insert banana dish apple pail.**

This may not seem like a very well-made sentence, but
it does show two separate actions in a single series of signs.
Sarah did not misread the sentence and insert the banana,
the dish *and* the apple in the pail. Her teachers felt that
the sentence proved Sarah understood several grammatical
rules, just as she understood that two colors needed a plural
verb. She knew that the subject, **Sarah**, acted on the verb
(by **inserting**) twice, even if **Sarah** was only spelled out
once. The verb, **insert**, controlled what happened to both
of the fruits, **banana** and **apple**, even if it too was only used
a single time. Sarah proved her understanding of compound
sentences when she turned **Randy give apple Sarah, Randy
give orange Sarah** and **Randy give banana Sarah** into the

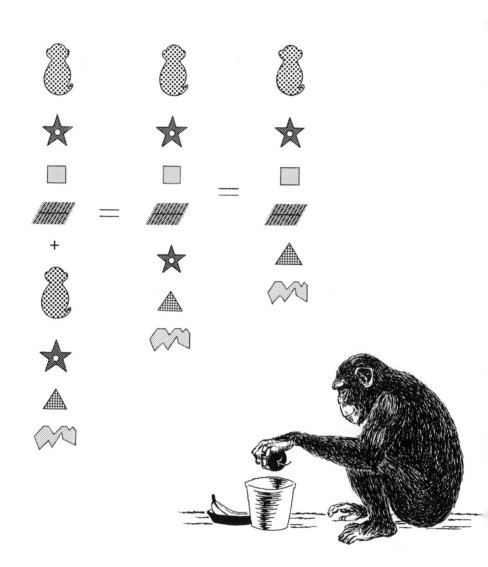

Steps leading to the compound sentence, **Sarah insert banana dish apple pail.**

Amounts

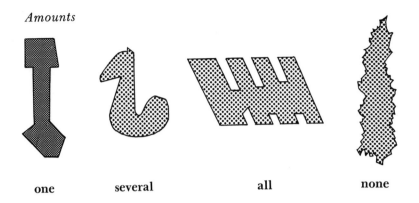

one   several   all   none

one greedy request, **Randy give apple orange banana Sarah.**

Amounts. Introducing Sarah to the idea of quantities was the next step in her carefully organized education. She was taught symbols for **all** and **none**, **several** and **one**, and then was tested by a long series of commands telling her to place different amounts of candy or crackers in a dish. Whenever she followed the directions correctly, the chimp was allowed to eat what was in the dish as a reward. After Sarah had successfully put in the dish **one cracker**, **several candy**, **one candy**, **several cracker**, and so on, she was told **Sarah insert none cracker dish.** She obeyed and did not add any crackers, but slyly slipped in a piece of candy, instead. Sarah also followed the next instruction, **Sarah insert several cracker dish**, but then she added *all* of the candy, grabbed the full dish and ran away with her prize. That was the end of the candy—and of the test!

If-then sentences. Some people still cannot believe that an ape can think logically. The same people agree that a child uses his mind logically when he understands *"If you*

Sarah

take

orange

if-then

Mary

give

candy

Sarah

If-then sentences

don't eat your spinach, *then* you won't get any dessert." Not having dessert is the logical result of not eating the spinach. The two phrases in the sentence depend on each other to make sense.

Sarah also learned that *if* she did something, *then* something else would follow. Her trainers used a single sign for the words "if" and "then" to make it easier for the chimp, and because they were trying to get the *idea* across to her, not the vocabulary. She was shown the sentence **Sarah take apple if-then** (the only new sign) **Mary give Sarah chocolate**. This meant "If Sarah takes the apple [she did], then Mary will give her chocolate [and Sarah got another reward]." The next sentence was **Sarah take banana if-then Mary no give Sarah chocolate**.

Later, Sarah's trainers reversed the fruits and spelled out two sentences promising the chimp her favorite chocolate if she took the banana, but not if she selected the apple. Sarah was used to picking the apple. She did it twenty times in a row without getting the reward she expected. Then she had a temper tantrum. When she calmed down, though, the chimp studied the signs very carefully and chose the right fruit to earn her chocolate at last.

After five years of training, Sarah used 130 symbols accurately about eighty percent of the time. Her vocabulary was roughly equal to that of a two-year-child.

Sarah also proved to the scientists that a chimpanzee's mind can sometimes work like a human's. A person seeing the word "apple," pictures a round, red fruit in his mind, not the letters *A*, *P*, *P*, *L*, and *E*. When Sarah was asked to describe the small, blue triangle, she called it large, red and

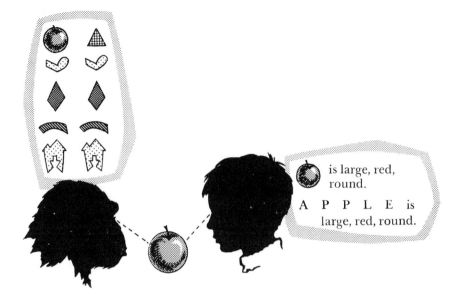

is large, red, round.

A P P L E is large, red, round.

round. The symbol for apple *was* an apple for the chimp.

This ability to transfer the *idea* of something from the real object to a word—or symbol—was once thought something that only the highly developed human mind could do. Washoe, as well as Sarah, was able to make this transfer. For Washoe a dog, a picture of one in her books and the sign for **dog** were the same thing. She did not like dogs, and she bristled in anger at the sign as well as at the sight of the real animal.

Sarah had learned to "read" and "write" in the plastic language of her symbols, and she used the symbols according to the rules of English grammar. With her regular lessons and the strict word order she was taught, this chimp seems more like a student at school, compared to Washoe, who was more like a child at home, "chatting" freely with her constant companions. Although the affection of her trainers was also important to Sarah, and she lost interest in her lessons if they did, she had less chance to express her personality. Washoe signed whatever came into her chimpanzee mind, while Sarah struggled with symbols and rules made up by human beings.

Dr. Premack believes that Sarah's education, and further work with other chimpanzees, can give valuable clues to brain function in people as well as in apes. How does a mind react to a situation, store the information it receives, and then bring it out of its "memory bank" instantly when it is needed and apply it to another situation? A baby who has been burned trying to touch a flame has the fact that fire hurts stored in his brain and always ready to warn him when he sees another flame. Chimpanzees and other animals also fear fire. In learning, retaining and then reusing this information, do their brains act as ours do?

Dr. Premack's experiments have already proved important to people in another way. His system of dividing language into simple, step-by-step lessons has been used to teach children and adults with brain damage. Sarah's logical, simple language might help everyone learn the illogical English language. Spelling would certainly be easier if one letter made all words plural, and there was no confusion about "-s," "-es" or "-ies."

Bruno and Booee—
and Washoe Again

Washoe and Sarah were communicating with people! But were they freaks—geniuses among apes? Could other chimpanzees be trained in sign language?

Dr. Roger Fouts, at the University of Oklahoma's Institute for Primate Studies, decided to try to teach four chimpanzees ten signs from Washoe's vocabulary—**hat, shoe, food, fruit, drink, look, listen, key, string** and **more.** He kept careful records of the experiment so that he could compare each animal's performance with that of the other three—and with Washoe. All four were older than Washoe had been when she began her training.

There were two males born in captivity and raised with humans for a good part of their lives, Bruno and Booee. Bruno was thirty-two months old and Booee, three years. The two females, Thelma and Cindy, were captured in the wild, so the scientists had to guess their ages. Cindy was about three years old, and Thelma probably four.

Like Sarah, the four chimpanzees were taught by one trainer and had regular lessons in a cage. Unlike Washoe, they were not surrounded by people all the time. The training sessions were as long as thirty minutes each, repeated one to three times a day, five days a week. But if one ape seemed nervous or excited, his lesson was shortened or dropped altogether.

The teacher shaped the chimps' hands into the proper positions for the signs they were learning. This method had been the most successful one with Washoe. With nine of the signs the chimpanzees were also shown an object that matched it—a ticking watch for **listen**, eyeglasses for **look** and, of course, a hat for **hat**. The tenth sign, **more**, was

*Booee names a piece of orange with the sign for **fruit**.*

combined with others. Its meaning became clear when the chimps were offered **more fruit** or **more drink**.

Dr. Fouts noted how long it took the animals to learn each different sign. The easiest one turned out to be **listen**. Bruno mastered it in only two minutes, while Thelma, the slowest of the chimps, took fifteen. The hardest sign was **string**. The different animals needed from just over two hours to almost nine hours training before they knew that one.

Although Bruno did well on **listen**, Booee was usually the quickest animal. This surprised the scientists, since the chimp had been used in medical research before he came to Oklahoma. The two halves of his brain had been separated by surgery. This did not slow Booee down at all. It took him an average of fifty-four minutes to learn each of the ten signs, while Cindy spent seventy-eight, Bruno 136 and poor Thelma 159.

When the animals seemed to know their lessons, the scientists set up tests to find out how well they recognized the objects and how regularly they used the right signs. Would the chimps who had learned the fastest also be the best in applying their signs?

The tests were like the double-blind ones that had been given to Washoe. A chimpanzee inside the training cage could see into a double-ended box in which the objects were put by someone outside the cage. Two observers, one in the cage and one outside, both unable to see what was in the box, judged the chimp's signs.

The observers could not reward the chimps with the usual praise or fruit, since they could not tell if the animals had made the right signs until the tests were finished. Without rewards, at least two of the apes did not do as well as expected.

Cindy had the lowest score, but she was a shy and insecure animal who needed extra amounts of affection and encouragement while she was learning the signs. During her training, people passing by the cage stopped to clap their hands and urge her on with "Good Cindy, good Cindy!" She lost interest in the tests when her trainer did not praise her, and only named twenty-six percent of the objects correctly.

Bright Booee, the one who learned most rapidly despite his divided brain, had the second lowest score, fifty-eight percent. But Booee was also a very greedy young chimpanzee. He did not do well without raisins and apples.

Slow-to-learn Thelma did better, using the proper sign almost sixty percent of the time. She was very easily distracted, though, and this held her back in both training and testing. For her, a fly in her cage was as interesting, or more so, than a shoe in a box.

Bruno was not insecure, like Cindy—greedy, like Booee—or absentminded—like Thelma. He had been hard to teach at first, because he just would not make the signs, even after his trainers changed his rewards from raisins to apples—to bananas—and finally, to soda. But he got to work right away after a teacher frowned and spoke to him harshly. On the tests he scored an impressive ninety percent. For one chimp, at least, a threat worked better than affection or rewards.

Almost all the mistakes the chimpanzees made were in

The apes made most of their mistakes during tests in the signs for **look**, **listen** *and* **key**, *all of which use the index finger.*

signs that resembled each other in subject matter or gesture. Like Washoe, they used **fruit** for **food**, or **drink** for **fruit**. They also confused **listen**, **look** and **key**, probably because all these signs used an index finger. A chimp should put the finger on his ear for **listen**, near an eye for **look** and in the palm of the other for **key**.

Bruno, Booee, Cindy and Thelma were part of a colony of chimpanzees at the farm of Dr. William Lemmon, the director of the Primate Institute. Different kinds of monkeys and twenty-four chimps lived there in several buildings and outdoor cages. One of the chimpanzees was Washoe.

A number of the research associates who had worked with Washoe had finished their studies in 1970. That left the Gardners without enough experienced chimpanzee workers, and it became impossible to keep Washoe in Nevada. Dr. Fouts, one of the graduating students who had helped with the ape, flew with Washoe to Oklahoma on a private plane, chartered just so the chimp would not have to live through the discomfort and neglect animals often suffer on regular flights. He stayed in Oklahoma and worked with Bruno, Booee, Thelma and Cindy, and with male and

Washoe, now at the farm in Oklahoma, wants Dr. Fouts to **go**.

female chimps of all ages, sometimes as many as three at one time. Washoe continued to learn, too, and increased her vocabulary to over 160 signs.

Washoe was lonely for all her human companions at first. She had not seen any fellow chimpanzees since infancy, and dismissed the unfamiliar apes as **bugs**. She signed **come**, **out** and **hug** repeatedly. But, when she became adjusted to living with the other animals, the always hungry chimp's favorite signs were again the usual **food, drink** and **hurry please**. They did not work as well as they once had, though, since Washoe had grown very fat from all the rewards she had earned by her successful signing, and had been put on a diet.

When the greedy chimp wanted a treat and Dr. Fouts refused, she called him **Dirty Roger**. Originally she had used **dirty** as a noun for something soiled, but she changed it to an adjective one day after an argument with a macaque. She was in a monkey house with Dr. Fouts, who was busy making notes, when she threatened the macaque. That angry monkey threatened back. Dr. Fouts stopped the quarrel and took Washoe over to a cage of siamangs. He wanted to teach her the sign for **monkey**, and practiced it with her until she began to call the siamangs **monkey**. Then he asked her what was in a cage of squirrel monkeys, and she answered with her new sign. But when Dr. Fouts showed her the macaque and asked **What that?** she described her enemy as **Dirty monkey**.

Washoe continued to use signs her own way. On the farm there was a pond surrounding some small islands. In good weather some of the chimps were rowed over to an island where they could play freely among the bare trunks of trees they had stripped during their games. A cross pair of swans patrolled the pond. Dr. Fouts pointed them out to Washoe as **ducks**. But she decided they were not ducks at all, and named them **water birds**—a better description!

Chimpanzee Children

Bruno had not always lived in the colony of chimpanzees at the University of Oklahoma. He spent two years in the home of a human family, until his care became too much for his "parents." After his arrival back at the colony, his trainers gave Bruno special attention. They brought him to their homes for visits to make the change from adoptee to orphan less sudden.

At the same time other chimpanzees were still living with their patient human families. Like babies, they had their own clothing, toys, beds and high chairs. They slept in their parents' rooms, played with other children in their families and went with them on trips. The little chimps ate at the table with silverware and were taught manners. The parents were also responsible for toilet training and disciplining the mischievous apes when their pranks got out of hand.

Dr. Lemmon, the director of the colony, was interested in comparing the development of these chimpanzees with the ones living in the colony. What behavior was so much a part of the nature of apes that it would show up in both babies raised by their animal mothers and ones who never saw another ape, but lived a life as close to a human child's as possible? It was the same question that had fascinated Dr. Kellogg. How much of a chimpanzee's development was controlled by heredity—the fact that he was an ape—and how much by environment—the human surroundings in which he grew?

The adopted chimps' lives could not be exactly like a baby's, since some changes had to be made in the homes where they scampered. There could be no curtains or standing lamps or other "branches" for the animal acrobats to climb. Plastic covers offered sensible protection for the furniture. Many things had to be locked away before the curious chimpanzees took them apart or broke them. Of course, keys themselves were also objects of curiosity. Locks were changed often to give the parents some privacy—and to keep their ape babies safe when they were left alone.

One specially bright and curious chimpanzee, Lucy, born in 1966, has spent most of her life with her family, Dr. and Mrs. Maurice Temerlin and their son, Steve. When she was a little over four and a half years old, Dr. Fouts began to visit her in her home to give her sign language lessons. He spent about two hours a day with her, practicing signs and playing games. First they "talked" about different things for which Lucy knew the signs—**dolls** and **brushes**, **pipes** and **beads**. More signs were called for when they went into the kitchen and sipped cups of tea together. Lucy liked to order Dr. Fouts around—in signs. **Comb Roger** meant that the friendly scientist had to comb his hair.

When Lucy decided **Out Lucy**, the games continued out-of-doors. **Hurry open car** earned her a ride—and maybe the sight of a dog or two, one of her favorite treats. The games and rides not only gave Lucy a chance to use her signs, but also kept her from becoming restless during the necessary business of learning new signs and practicing her old vocabulary.

In six weeks Lucy learned as many signs as Washoe had in her first eighteen weeks of training, and she knew ninety-seven by the summer of 1974. Like Washoe, she also invented signs. She surprised her family one time by holding her hooked finger next to her neck. They decided she was describing her **leash**—and suggesting a walk.

Lucy shared Washoe's ability to divide things into categories. During one study, she was given twenty-four different fruits and vegetables to play with—or eat—and to name with her signs. At that time she knew five signs concerned with food—**fruit, banana, candy, drink** and **food** itself. Lucy regularly named **fruit** with the proper sign more often than with **food**, but vegetables were more often **food** than **fruit**.

Lucy described the foods as well as named them. Watermelon was **candy drink** or **drink fruit**, while a juicy tomato was **drink food**. **Smell fruit** meant all the tangy citruses—oranges, lemons, limes and grapefruit. After a bite of radish Lucy was sure it was a **cry hurt food**. Celery sticks

Lucy signs **hurt** *by bringing her fingertips together at the spot that was hurt. The flower at her feet helped her practice that sign earlier in her lesson.*

and pickles, nibbled at one end with the rest sticking out from the mouth, reminded her of **pipes**.

As Lucy grew older, it became difficult for the Temerlins to spend much time with her during the day. Steve was in high school, and both his parents worked at the Institute. To give the ape a chance for exercise and fresh air, the Temerlins built a cage on the roof. A stair, also barred, led to Lucy's room, so she was able to amuse herself either indoors or out. When Mrs. Temerlin returned home after the first time Lucy had been alone all day, the ape sulked and ignored her. She greeted Dr. Temerlin and Steve and some dinner guests with enthusiasm. She played with the adults and wrestled with Steve, but still paid no attention to her mother. Only after dinner, which the chimp ate at the table with her family and their guests, did she forgive Mrs. Temerlin and curl up in her lap for a nap.

Lucy enjoyed visitors, and whatever the visitors brought with them. A woman's handbag gave the curious chimp a fine chance to explore. Lucy emptied it, sniffed the perfume and patted her nose with the powder puff, while staring at herself in the compact mirror. After Lucy had investigated everything thoroughly, she put it all back in place carefully and closed the purse with its zipper.

Sign language became such a natural part of Lucy's life that she even tried to teach it. Once she placed her pet cat between her knees facing her. While the cat watched, Lucy pointed to a book and then signed **book**, repeatedly but unsuccessfully.

Another home-raised chimp, Ally, born in 1969, lived with Sherri Roush. Dr. Fouts started teaching him sign

Friendly Ally offers to share his supper with the cat. From *Science Year, The World Book Science Annual.* © 1973 Field Enterprises Educational Corporation.

language when he was a little more than a year old, and by 1973 he had mastered seventy signs. Freckle-faced Ally was even more active than most young apes. Although he made very clear signs, he preferred to scoot around the room, turn somersaults or bounce on the sofa. His teacher had to catch him by his shirt to hold the little animal still long enough to answer a question.

Unlike Washoe, chimps living in homes heard English spoken all the time. They learned to understand a good many words. Dr. Fouts and two graduate students wondered if Ally could learn *both* the word and the sign for the same

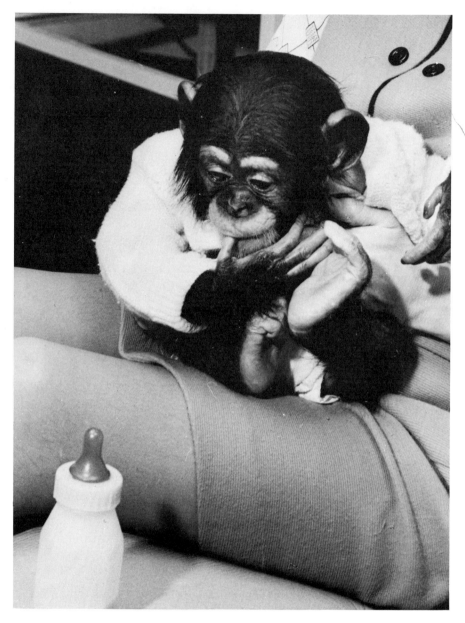

The sight of her bottle tempts little Salome to sign **drink**.

thing. First, they taught him the word "spoon" with a spoon as the example. Next, they trained him to make the sign for **spoon** by using just the word, not a spoon itself, during his lessons. They said "spoon" while shaping his hands properly, or asked "Sign spoon" or even made the gesture for **sign** and then spoke "spoon."

Later, Ally had no trouble using the sign to name a real spoon, even though he had learned it from the word "spoon." He knew the piece of silverware was the same as *both* the sign and the word. You might amost say that Ally knew two languages!

Lucy and the other chimpanzees who picked up signs more rapidly than Washoe started their training when they were older than she had been. The older chimps were able to practice their lessons for a longer time than the little ones without a recess for a romp or wrestling match with their teachers. They also could control their hands better as they grew up. But one very little chimpanzee learned to ask for **food** by the time she was four months old.

Salome was born in the summer of 1971 and lived with Churchill and Susie Blakey, their baby daughter, Robin, and their large, shaggy dog. At an age when human infants can only cry, Salome had learned **drink**, too. She could tell her family if she was hungry or wanted her bottle. At twenty-one months, the bright baby ape began to put her fifteen signs together in short phrases—the familiar **Gimme food**, **Gimme drink** and **You tickle me**.

Lana in a Plastic Cube

Compared to Salome's cozy childhood, an ape at the Yerkes Regional Primate Center called Lana Chimpanzee seems to lead a life right out of science fiction. Lana is the star of the latest experiment in communicating with chimps, an experiment led by Dr. Duane M. Rumbaugh of the Department of Psychology at Georgia State University.

The four-year-old chimp has lived for two years in a seven-by-seven-foot room with transparent plastic walls. On one wall there are two dispensers for liquids, three for food, and two loudspeakers for broadcasting music. Lana's transparent "learning environment" is set inside a larger room that has screens for movies and slide shows and a window to the outdoors—plus a computer.

The most important thing in Lana's life is a computer panel on one wall of her room, like a vertical typewriter keyboard. It has large keys one inch high and an inch and a half wide. Each key is marked with a design that stands for a word. The chimp presses the keys to "talk" to the computer, or, through the computer, to a person in the outer room. There, the experimenter also has a control panel on which he can punch out messages that the computer passes on to Lana.

Lana uses her machine day and night to get food, drink or entertainment for herself. During the day she can ask the operator outside to come into her room and tickle her. At all times, she can tell her machine to give her something to eat or perhaps some fruit juice, which she guzzles through a metal tube from one of the closed containers for liquids. Lana wakes during the night to demand a sip of water, a little music or a chance to see herself and her trainers, or

Lana's "learning environment," inside a larger room.

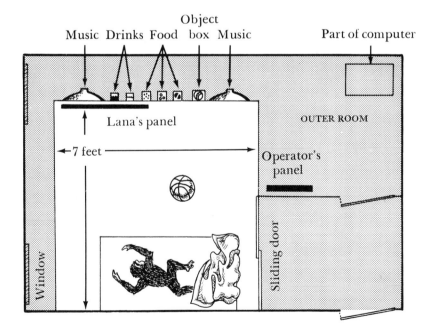

other apes and people, in the slides and movies. At dawn the chimp seems to feel the growing light. She repeatedly punches out **Please machine make window open period.** Each time she asks, Lana gets a thirty-second peek at the out-doors. Her music, slides and movies are also rationed into thirty-second periods.

The complicated computer system, and the language it teaches, were designed by an impressive team of scientists and computer specialists. The language they invented is called "Yerkish." Like Ameslan and Sarah's symbols, it is a visual language. The "words" are geometric designs. All the designs are made from nine basic patterns, which can be used alone or overlapped to make a total of 255 possible designs, named "lexigrams." For example, the lexigram for **nut** contains three of the nine patterns:

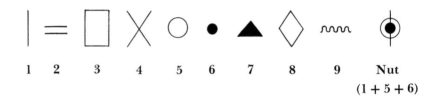

1	2	3	4	5	6	7	8	9	Nut
									(1 + 5 + 6)

Lana's lexigrams are painted different colors as a clue to the categories in which they belong. There are red lexigrams for food and drink, violet for living beings, including humans, blue for activities and four other colors for other word groups.

English is hard for foreigners to learn because there are often several meanings for the same word. In Yerkish, each lexigram stands for just one idea. **Groom** means only groom-

Lana has read her trainer's message, **Question Lana groom Tim,** *on the projectors and is answering.*

Lana grooming Timothy Gill after replying to his request with **Yes,** *a blank button without any lexigram design. It shows on the far left projector and on the button at lower right.*

ing the chimp—or Lana grooming her trainer. It does not also cover a stablehand or a man about to be married. Just a sample of the synonyms for "stick" in the dictionary includes "branch," "club," "cane," "bat," "pole," "stab," "prick," "puncture," "cling," "insert," "paste" and "glue." For Lana, a **stick** is only one thing—a long, thin, solid object. If she were ever treated to a peppermint stick, another lexigram would have to be made for the candy.

In English, all the different ways words are arranged in sentences can be confusing, too. If you see the sentence "The man was killed by a rock," you do not know if the rock actually cracked his skull, or if something else killed him while he was just standing *near* the rock. To keep Lana's language simple, only the direct order of subject-verb-object is allowed. Each subject can be used only with certain verbs, and each verb only with certain objects. "Lana eats milk" is correct grammar in English, even if it seems a little silly, but not in Yerkish. **Give milk** and **drink milk** are correct combinations for the computer. **Eat milk** is not.

There is room on Lana's keyboard for 125 lexigrams, and she knew seventy-five by late 1973. If she learns more than 125 signs, they will be alternated, with part of her vocabulary on the board at one time and another part at another. Even now, the designs are moved every day, so that Lana cannot push the right key just by remembering where it is on the board.

When the chimp is learning new lexigrams, or practicing her sentence structure, the keys not needed in the lesson are "dead"—or deactivated—temporarily. Active keys are faintly lit from the back, and this draws Lana's attention to the ones needed in her lesson. When she actually pushes a key, the light behind it glows more brightly.

Above Lana's keyboard are two rows of miniature TV screens where the signs she selects are shown from left to right almost immediately after she presses the keys. If she makes a mistake, the computer either makes a noise meaning "error" or turns off the projection of the sentence. Lana can erase her words herself by pushing the **period** key, which shows that her statement is completed. Then the screens are cleared for further communications. If the chimp does not bother to finish a sentence properly, the computer waits a little while and then removes the signs.

On his own keyboard outside the plastic cube, the observer can give orders to Lana, or ask questions, which the computer then projects on Lana's screens for the chimp to read. The hard-working machine types all communications, day and night, on tapes. These printouts also show whether the sentence was made by the human operator or the chimpanzee.

After just a week in her plastic world, Lana could supply herself with food, drink or candy by telling her machine **Please chow** (monkey-food)—or **M&M** or **milk**—**period**.

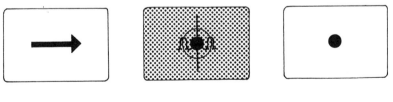

| Please | M&M | period |

Learning Yerkish

During the very first days in her computerized home, Lana earned a reward if she pushed just a single key, such as **M&M**. Then she was taught to start with **please**—not because the scientists wanted a chimp with beautiful manners, but because **please** was a signal to the computer that a request was on the way. **Period** at the end of a sentence was also information for the computer, not an attempt to teach the chimp punctuation. It meant that the statement was finished and the signs for it could be erased from the screens.

The scientists who had developed this complicated training system were not sure how to teach Lana the connection between the keys she pressed and the pictures on the screens above. Lana solved the problem herself. Even though the pictures were larger than the keyboard lexigrams, and their colors slightly different from the ones on the keys, the little chimp grasped the relationship between her "typewriter" and the sentence it produced without help.

When Lana pushed **M&M**, she was using just one "word" to express a whole sentence, like a baby saying "Cookie" before he is able to ask, "Mother, may I have a cookie, please?" This one word substitute for a complete thought is called a "hologram" by scientists. Lana's trainers taught her step-by-step to stretch her holograms into sentences. The first sentence they worked toward was **Please machine give M&M period**. This whole sentence was always spelled out on Lana's screens, even when she was just using a few of the signs, so that she would become familiar with all the lexigrams and their proper order.

At first, Lana was rewarded for just **M&M**, but then she had to use **please** and **period** also. She earned her treat if she put her **please** first and **period** last, with any of the other three words in the center. **Please machine period**, **Please give period** or **Please M&M period** all inspired the computer to drop a little candy in the dispenser. Later, Lana received her M&M only if she used four signs, **Please —— M&M period**. Either **machine** or **give** could fill the gap. Finally, she had to punch the keys for all five words, **Please machine give M&M period**. When Lana could do this, she was taught the structure of new sentences by the same method of adding one lexigram at a time. Then the chimp was able to exchange other lexigrams for ones in the sentence structures and ask for **milk** or **chow** as well as **M&Ms**.

The scientists provided the chimp with a **question** lexigram, which could be used to start sentences in place of **please**. This lexigram is the familiar question mark, one of

After asking **Please machine make slides,** *Lana points to a picture of her favorite M & Ms.*

the few not made out of the nine basic patterns. **Question** told the computer what was coming, just as **please** warned it to expect a request. And, of course, Lana learned **yes** and **no** so that she could answer questions.

With the new design Lana's teachers could ask her, through their own keyboard, **Question name of this period,** with samples of fruits or candy. Lana read their questions on her screens, but it took two weeks, or 1,600 trials, before she learned to answer correctly **Banana** (or **M&M**) **name of this period.** Once the chimpanzee realized that objects had names, she caught on more quickly with other samples. The very first time she was asked to name **ball, blanket** and **milk,** she succeeded. Then she began to name the food she ate spontaneously and conversationally, and to comment **Movie name of this period** or **Slide name of this period.** Finally, the clever chimp began to question her trainers about the names of new objects they brought into her room. Her curiosity led her to ask for abstract information—a name—as well as for real rewards, like her M&Ms.

Washoe and Lucy invented signs and Lana also proved that she could make up a name by herself. Not knowing the lexigram for an orange, she asked for the **apple which-is orange.**

By 1974, Lana knew five other colors and was learning the meaning of prepositions like **in, out** and **behind.**

Lana invented her own sentences to cope with changing situations. At night, when there were no people at the keyboard to read her requests, the printouts showed that the lonely chimp asked her computer for company—**Please machine tickle come into room period**—poor Yerkish grammar because **Machine tickle** was impossible.

| Question | name-of | this | period |

| Blanket | name-of | this |

Although the computer could not go in and play with her, Lana's life was not as empty as it might seem. Three trainers worked and played with her during the day. They groomed or tickled the chimp, swung her by her arms or joined her in games of ball. When a teacher was in Lana's room, he punched out questions or suggestions for games on the chimp's own keyboard. Then in turn, Lana scampered across the room to answer his message with the keys. She could also use two sentences that earned her a chance to go outside.

Lana also enjoyed climbing and swinging on bars in her cubicle. While she was hanging from one right above the screens, the chimp sometimes accidentally hit one of the keys on the board below. If she hit just any sign, she erased it by pressing **period**. But, if she happened to press **please**, she took advantage of her mistake and added lexigrams for food or drink. Lana was "reading" the screens and "writing" on them, through the keys, cleverly and accurately.

To test Lana's ability to read and to follow the computer's rules, the scientists started different phrases on the screens for the chimp to complete. Some of them could be continued into proper sentences and some of them were nonsense, so that the computer would reject them if Lana tried to finish them. Among the nonsense phrases were **Please groom machine—**, **Please movie blanket—** and **Please bite milk—**. Lana erased ninety percent of these by firmly pushing **period**. However, she finished ninety-four percent of the beginning phrases that were good Yerkish grammar.

Dr. Rumbaugh and his associates did not just want to talk with apes. They felt that chimpanzees had a much greater intelligence than they needed for their simple jungle life. The scientists hoped that a sophisticated, man-made system would catch the animals' interest and help their communication with humans to develop as much as possible.

So far, Lana seems to be learning Yerkish easily. If she starts to have trouble, the scientists can change her "language" and rewire the computer. The new language would be based on what they were learning about the workings of a chimpanzee mind, not a human one. Dr. Rumbaugh also believes that a computer programmed to the abilities of retarded people could be used to teach them in the same way.

Meanwhile, the musical taste of chimpanzees, or of at least one chimpanzee, may soon be known. Lana is treated to a burst of loud rock when she asks her machine for **music**, but, as her lexigram vocabulary grows, she will be given a chance to choose jazz or classical music instead.

Scientists flash nonsense phrase on projectors, **Please banana bite.**
Lana understands and firmly pushes **period** *to erase the nonsense.*

What Next?

At about the time that Lana moved into her plastic home in Georgia, the Gardners were starting another project in Nevada. These new experiments solved two of the problems that had limited Washoe's accomplishments—her teachers' inexperience with sign language and the age of the chimp when her training began.

The Gardners visited colleges for the deaf to speak and show movies of Washoe. Interested students, students who had been using sign language themselves all their lives, volunteered to work with the chimpanzees.

It also proved possible to get newborn chimps who could be exposed to signs from their very first days. Moja arrived in Reno just one day after she was born, on November 18, 1972. The infant chimp needed the same care as a human baby. There were diaperings and feedings, with sterilized bottles, night and day, and inoculations against disease. However, Moja could not be left in her crib for long periods of time, as human babies are, since chimpanzee mothers hold and handle their offspring constantly. So when her trainers were too busy to cuddle Moja, she was kept close to them by riding in a baby carrier, like an Indian papoose.

During her very early months, Moja could hold toys, use finger paints and recognize the difference between her friends and strangers. Her first signs were seen when she was almost three months old. By the time she was six months, she was using fifteen. This is not as advanced as it seems. Human babies have been recorded making recognizable signs between their fifth and sixth months. Most mothers probably do not notice these repeated gestures, though, since they are eagerly waiting for a first word instead.

Five-month-old Nina already has her own gesture for "gimme"—not Ameslan, but easy to understand.

The Gardners are using the same recording system as they did with Washoe, but the records will be more complete. It took some time to develop the best methods with Washoe, but now the perfected system can be used with new chimpanzees from the moment they arrive. One 20-minute sample of Moja's communication, taken while she was being fed and tickled when she was about four months old, showed that she signed thirty-one times, using six different signs. Moja only wanted a **drink** once, but **come-gimme** was repeated seventeen times.

The Gardners plan to continue their experiments with more chimpanzees, starting with a new baby about each year. A second chimp, Pili, has already arrived at the University. He and Moja will grow up together like children in the same family. The Gardners hope that the "big sister" will help teach her "little brother." Inexperienced research associates will work with the infant chimps until they are ready to handle older apes and more complicated record-keeping. Then new students, in turn, will care for and learn from the babies. With a constant supply of experienced chimpanzee workers to help, the Gardners will be able to continue the animals' educations for longer than they could with Washoe.

In California, Sarah became impossible to work with after she was fully grown. Adult chimps weigh about 120 pounds, although some individuals may be even heavier. But they are three to five times as strong as a man of the same size. Chimpanzees take their mistakes seriously. One who puts the wrong symbol on the board is apt to have a temper tantrum. And a tantrum by an animal with the strength of a 360- to 600-pound man is dangerous! Without wanting to hurt his trainer, the ape can still cause a great deal of damage with his flailing arms.

Sarah's successors are Peony, close to three years old, and Elizabeth, about four. Dr. Premack found that they were very slow, as Sarah had been, in understanding their first word. In the beginning, they seemed to learn the wrong things. Peony, after she had always been shown one fruit and had put a symbol on the board to earn it, was then given an apple and a banana to choose from, with a symbol already on the board. She was supposed to select the fruit that matched the sign. Instead, she picked up the

Eight-month-old "little brother," Pili, romps with his "big sister," Moja.

banana, smeared it across the board and then tried to eat what was left. For Peony, putting something on the board was the path to rewards, not pairing signs and objects. Once the chimpanzees understood the structure of their new language—that one plastic piece meant one fruit or other object—their vocabularies increased quickly. The first step was the hardest one.

Peony and Elizabeth are also being trained to use a typewriter with keys marked with the shapes and colors of the "words" in their plastic language.

Meanwhile, exciting news has come from the colony at Dr. Lemmon's farm in Oklahoma. Chimpanzees usually take very good care of their babies. Even strong, old males will let young ones in their group slap and tease them. But when Washoe arrived, she was not used to chimpanzee ways and she bullied the little apes. The other adults ganged up on her when she misbehaved, until she learned to treat the babies more naturally. In time, Washoe became a very motherly animal, comforting sick youngsters and defending ones picked on by other apes. Once, when she was on the island with a group of chimps, they saw a snake in the grass. Chimpanzees are terrified of snakes. They all fled except Washoe and young Bruno. He had not seen the reptile. Washoe first signed to him **Come hug hurry, come hug hurry**, urging him away from the danger. When the younger ape paid no attention, Washoe gave up signing and dragged him to safety. The chimpanzee not only used signs with her trainers, but also with other animals!

Much of the time Washoe was frustrated when she tried to sign to her fellow apes. None of them had a vo-

Ally, now back in the chimpanzee colony, signs **you** *to Bruno.*

cabulary anywhere near her 160 signs. Dr. Fouts is studying Bruno and Booee, each of whom know about forty signs. The two chimps respond to each other's requests for comfort—**Come hug**—and fun—**Come tickle.** If one is eating or drinking, though, he will ignore his comrade's hopeful **Gimme fruit** or **Gimme drink!** One time Booee suggested to Bruno **Tickle Booee.** The other chimp was busy eating raisins from the hand of one of the students. He motioned **Booee me food**, probably meaning, "No, Booee, I'm eating." Bruno went back to his raisins, and poor Booee did not get a tickling.

After completing his studies of the communication between the two chimps, Dr. Fouts plans to add Washoe to the group. Will Bruno and Booee learn signs from the more advanced ape? Will Washoe be able to tell her human friends the meaning of the other apes' animal sounds, translating from "chimpanzee" into Ameslan?

Washoe is also nearing the age when she can mate. There is a great deal of curiosity among the scientists about whether she would teach her new language to her baby.

By studying the apes' learning of language, Dr. Fouts hopes to find clues to the development of speech in human beings. It is possible that our early ancestors first used sign language to communicate. As primitive people developed, words might have accompanied some of the gestures. Then, after a period of time during which the two languages overlapped, speech became the most important one. Signs have never completely disappeared from human communication, though. Not only the deaf, but clowns in the circus and pantomimists on the stage, as well as frantic tourists in foreign countries, can get their messages across without speech.

Anyone lucky enough to live in Portland, Oregon, can watch chimps being taught sign language—and learn a little themselves. Dr. Philip Ogilvie, the director of the Portland Zoological Gardens, is trying to make the animals' lives in cement cages more interesting—and to make the animals more interesting to the visiting people. Different kinds of monkeys earn treats by working with lights and levers. Elephants, camels, giraffes, seals and ostriches have learned that they can get extra food if they push lighted buttons with their noses or beaks or even chins.

Volunteers at the zoo are training chimpanzees in a

At the Portland Zoo, Patty West and Charlie sign **chase** *together before an interested audience.*

wire-netted cage where they can be seen by passersby, who often enjoy trying the signs themselves. One time a teacher got tired of playing with a chimp named Charlie by chasing him. The eager little ape signed **chase** to another chimp, Jezebel, and the game continued.

Chimpanzees, and human beings, are not the only animals who can use sign language. Dr. Fouts has also worked briefly with a baby orangutan. The infant learned the usual first signs, such as **drink**, **food** and **tickle**. He had started to combine them into phrases when Dr. Fouts had to drop the lessons because he did not have enough time.

Meanwhile, Francine Patterson of Stanford University started training a nineteen-month-old gorilla. Koco. He lives in a trailer equipped with swings and climbing bars. The very big baby knows those important signs—**food, drink** and **out**—and has begun to add **more** to these requests. Koco can also ask for **candy** with a finger on his cheek, or name a **flower.**

Koko, the gorilla, practices **mask,** *encouraged by her trainer, Francine Patterson.*

What the apes have accomplished is so outstanding that it is easy to overlook what they cannot do—and probably never will. They do not discuss what happened in the past or plan what to do tomorrow. They cannot write detailed instructions about how to play a game or solve a problem. And they do not tell stories about strange, talking people.

The limits of the chimpanzees' ability to use human language, however, have yet to be discovered. Would it be possible for an animal to both "speak" in signs and "read" and "write" as Sarah and Lana do? Ally learned the connection between the spoken "spoon" and the sign for it. Could he also be trained to use a plastic symbol or lexigram for the same word?

The apes understood the idea of "words" and learned to use their words effectively within frameworks based on the "grammar" of Ameslan, Yerkish or simplified English. Could less intelligent animals learn an even simpler form of communication? Dr. Premack has been working with dogs, trying to teach them that different shapes of wooden blocks stand for different types of meat—sausage, hamburger, bacon and fish. So far, he has had no success, but maybe the stories of "talking" dogs will come true some day.

As yet, no tame chimpanzee has ever been returned to the wild. If a jungle tribe accepted such an animal, would he be able to pass along his new language? Of course, he would have to know signs more appropriate to forest life than **cup**, **hat** and **car**. Could he make up signs, like Lucy's invention for **leash**, for things important to wild apes? It is

After seeing Bruno eating a piece of orange, Ally asks him for **food**, *in Washoese.*

Bruno generously feeds his friend a slice, perhaps because there is enough fruit for all.

exciting to think men might be able to give chimps a boost up the ladder of evolution.

With great imagination and patience, psychologists are exploring the apes' capabilities. The possibilities for the future are even more exciting than the fact that chimpanzees are actually "speaking" with men today.

Bibliography

Bourne, Geoffrey H. *The Ape People*. New York: G. P. Putnam's Sons, 1971.

Chasan, Daniel J. "In this zoo, visitors learn, but not more than animals." Washington: *Smithsonian*, July 1974.

Dembeck, Herman. *Willingly to School—How Animals Are Taught*. New York: Taplinger Publishing Co., 1972.

Fant, Louis J., Jr. *Ameslan—an Introduction to American Sign Language*. Maryland: National Association of the Deaf, 1972.

Farb, Peter. "People Are Talking," *Horizon*, Vol. XVI, No. 1, 1974.

Fouts, Roger S. "Acquisition and Testing of Gestural Signs in Four Young Chimpanzees." *Science*, June 1, 1973.

—"Talking with Chimpanzees." *Science Year*, 1973.

—"Capacities for Language in the Great Apes." *Proceedings of the IXth International Congress of Anthropological and Ethnological Science*. Hague: Mouton & Co., 1973 (in press).

—Correspondence. Dec., 1973, June, 1974.

Gardner, R. Allen and Beatrice T. "Two-way Communication with an Infant Champanzee." *Behavior of Non-Human Primates*, Vol. 4. New York: Academic Press, 1971.

—"Communication with a Young Chimpanzee: Washoe's Vocabulary." *Modeles animaux de comportement humain*, No. 198, 1972.

—*Psychobiology of Two-way Communication*, progress report. National Science Foundation, May, 1973.

—"Teaching Sign Language to a Chimpanzee." *Science*, August 15, 1973.

—"Language." *Yearbook of Science and Technology*. New York: McGraw-Hill. 1973.

—*Comparing the Early Utterances of Child and Chimpanzee*, Minnesota Symposium on Child Psychology, 1973 (in press).

—Telephone conversation with Dr. Allen Gardner, May 28, 1974.

Garner, Richard L., *Apes and Monkeys: Their Life and Language*. Boston: Ginn & Company, 1900.

Hahn, Emily. *On the Side of the Apes*. New York: Thomas Y. Crowell Co., 1971. (in paperback, New York: Arena Books, 1972.)

Hayes, Catherine. *The Ape in Our House*. New York: Harper & Row. 1951.

Kay, Helen. *The Secrets of the Dolphins*. New York: Macmillan Co., 1964.

Kellogg, Winthrop N. "Communication and Language in the Home-Raised Chimp." *Science*, Oct. 25, 1968.

Kellogg, Winthrop N. and L. A. *The Ape and the Child*. New York: Whittlesey House, 1933.

Lieberman, P., Crelin E., and Klatt, D., "Phonetic ability and related anatomy of the newborn and adult human, Neanderthal Man, and the chimpanzee," *American Anthropologist*, Vol. 74, 1972.

Lilly, John C. *The Mind of the Dolphin—a Nonhuman Intelligence*. New York: Doubleday and Co. 1967. (in paperback, New York: Avon Books, 1969.)

Premack, Ann J. and David. "Teaching Language to an Ape." *Scientific American*, Oct., 1972.

Premack, David. "Language in a Chimpanzee," *Science*, May 21, 1970.

—"Cognitive Principles" (reprint).

—Correspondence, Dec., 1973, June, 1974.

Rensberger, Boyce. "Computer Helps Chimpanzees Learn to Read, Write and Talk to Humans." *New York Times,* May, 29, 1974.

Rumbaugh, Duane M, von Glaserfeld, E. C., and Gill, T. V. "Reading and Sentence Completion by a Chimpanzee (Pan)." *Science,* Vol. 182, 1973.

—"Methods and Designs—a Computer-Controlled Language Training System for Investigating the Language Skills of Young Apes," *Behavior Research Methods and Instrumentation,* Vol. 5, 1973.

—"Lana (Chimpanzee) Learning Language," *Yerkes Newsletter,* 1974.

—Correspondence, April, 1974.

van Lawick-Goodall, Jane. *In the Shadow of Man.* Boston: Houghton Mifflin Co., 1971. (in paperback, New York: Dell Publishing Co., 1972.)

Suggestions for Further Reading

Bourne, Geoffrey H. *The Ape People*. New York: G. P. Putnam's Sons, 1971.

Cohen, Daniel. *Talking With Animals*. New York: Dodd, Mead & Co., 1971.

Dembeck, Herman. *Willingly to School—How Animals Are Taught*. New York: Taplinger Publishing Co., 1972.

Fant, Louis J., Jr. *Ameslan—an Introduction to American Sign Language*. Maryland: National Association of the Deaf, 1972.

Garner, Richard, *The Baboon*. New York: Macmillan Co., 1972.

Garner, Richard L. *Apes and Monkeys—Their Life and Language*. Boston: Ginn & Co, 1900.

Gray, Robert. *The Great Apes*. New York: W. W. Norton & Co., 1969.

Freedman, Russell and Morris, James E. *How Animals Learn*. New York: Holiday House, 1969.

Hahn, Emily. *On the Side of the Apes*. New York: Thomas Y. Crowell Co., 1971.

Hayes, Catherine. *The Ape in Our House*. New York: Harper & Row, 1951.

Kay, Helen. *Apes.* New York: Macmillan Co., 1970.

—*The Secrets of the Dolphins.* New York: Macmillan Co., 1964.

Kellogg, Winthrop N. and L. A. *The Ape and the Child.* New York: Whittlesey House, 1933.

van-Lawick-Goodall, Jane. *In the Shadow of Man.* Boston: Houghton Mifflin Co., 1971. (in paperback, New York: Dell Publishing Co., 1972.)

PHOTOGRAPH CREDITS